ST. MARY'S COLLEGE OF MARYLAND LIBRARY
ST. MARY'S

THE ESSENTIALS OF COMPOSITION
AS APPLIED TO ART

THE MACMILLAN COMPANY
NEW YORK · BOSTON · CHICAGO · DALLAS
ATLANTA · SAN FRANCISCO

MACMILLAN & CO., LIMITED
LONDON · BOMBAY · CALCUTTA
MELBOURNE

THE MACMILLAN CO. OF CANADA, LTD.
TORONTO

THE ESSENTIALS
OF COMPOSITION AS APPLIED
TO ART

BY

JOHN VREDENBURGH VAN PELT

ARCHITECTE DIPLOMÉ PAR LE GOUVERNEMENT FRANÇAIS; FORMER PROFESSOR
OF DESIGN AND PROFESSOR IN CHARGE IN THE COLLEGE OF ARCHI-
TECTURE, CORNELL UNIVERSITY; FORMER ASSOCIATE
STUDIO DIRECTOR, COLUMBIA UNIVERSITY

ILLUSTRATED BY THE AUTHOR

New York
THE MACMILLAN COMPANY
1913

All rights reserved

COPYRIGHT, 1902 AND 1913,

BY THE MACMILLAN COMPANY.

———

Set up and electrotyped. New edition. Published September, 1913.

Norwood Press
J. S. Cushing Co. — Berwick & Smith Co.
Norwood, Mass., U.S.A.

1240

PREFACE TO THE FIRST EDITION

PERSONS of various interests have asked me to recommend a work on Architecture as an Art. There was nothing that exactly met their requirements, and this suggested the idea of writing something myself. Although some of these pages are primarily for students of architecture, I hope the general public may find matter of interest in the book. Its first concrete form was a course of lectures I delivered at Cornell University, between the years 1897 and 1900.

The present Discussion of Composition is divided into six parts. The first treats the general laws of character in art; the second, general technical laws; the last four have to do with applications, three and five being, respectively, theoretical discussions of decoration and plan, four and six containing practical suggestions in the same subjects.

I cannot claim that much of this is my own conception, for Composition is the practice of Art, and Art is as old as Humanity. Where the source of the following pages is itself a written page I have referred the reader to the earlier writer (the latter may, in turn, direct him to a yet earlier origin). Some of these are Ruskin, Tolstoi, G. Baldwin Brown, Viollet le Duc, Mayeux, Müntz, Magne, Louis F. Day, and Helmholtz. Where the origin lies in the direct channel of student to instructor reference has been less easy. A great deal of part VI. of this volume is due to the teachings of M. J. Gaudet, Professor of the Theory of Architecture at the Ecole des Beaux Arts, Paris. To his name I would add, in paying homage, those of my chefs d'Atelier, MM. A. Thierry and Henri Deglane, sources of a more personal inspiration. It was M. Thierry who made me realize the significance of a plan ; M. Deglane taught me the meaning of the word " Composition." In particular, I desire to express my indebtedness to M. Deglane.

The illustrations in text are necessarily my own work : figure 33, an exception, was drawn from pencil sketches of mine, by M. Rapin. To MM. Pascal, Deglane, Tournaire, Chaussemiche, Bigot, and Duquesne I am indebted for their courtesy in allowing me to reproduce the " Grand Prix " plans.

JOHN V. VAN PELT.

Villino San Marino, Fiesole, Florence,
June 3, 1901.

PREFACE TO THE SECOND EDITION

In putting forth a new edition of the following work, the publishers and I have tried to find a name that would be more concise and more explicit than "Discussion of Composition." A decade has developed new methods of building which demanded recognition, and the past ten years of office practice have made it possible for me to introduce a few suggestions that may be useful to the young practitioner. Furthermore, science has progressed. The attitude of the medical profession and of experts in pedagogy is fostering a vogue for "open air" hospitals and schools, and for the outdoor life in general, while such subjects as acoustics have made marked advances. Of all this, it was necessary to take cognizance. Nevertheless, the essentials of Composition are intrinsically the same, and will remain the same until human nature itself changes. I hope, therefore, that the book in its new form may find as many friends as it has in the past.

JOHN V. VAN PELT.

New York City,
July 14, 1913.

CONTENTS

THE ESSENTIALS OF COMPOSITION
AS APPLIED TO ART

THE ESSENTIALS OF COMPOSITION
AS APPLIED TO ART

PART I

CHAPTER I

AN analysis of composition must needs be negative rather than positive. This results from the fact that while a production is not necessarily good because it complies with the laws of composition, it is surely faulty if it contradicts them. The following discussion will therefore be more filled with the cry "do not," than with that of "do"; but in spite of this, the reader must not think the writer a pessimist.

The term "composition," when taken apart from the phrase "laws of composition," may mean something more than a mere enchaining of elements. In our work we should strive for an artistic composition, and this interpretation I shall usually wish understood. Therefore, notwithstanding the fact that æstheticians of two centuries have split hairs on the subject, it would be well to agree on just what we mean by an artistic composition or work of art.

A work of art ! I wish to use the term in its broad-

B   1

est sense, viz. : It is that which, having been intention-
ally created, is capable of producing the sentiment or
impression aimed at by the artist, and in all persons
able to respond to such sentiments or impressions.
Thus, that which is intended to be beautiful should
seem beautiful to the observer or hearer. There are
works designed to produce certain impressions which
really produce quite opposite ones. These are failures.

The foregoing general definition of a work of art
admits, in its very broadness, many different kinds
or grades of such works. The small boy who invents
a clever lie, and, deceiving his parents, escapes a whip-
ping, has produced a work of art. Yet no one would
applaud such a production. Some paintings, their
subject being essentially sensual, evoke only a feeling
of pleasure in their color or line. Others stir our better
emotions. Also, some compositions are interesting
because they remind us of peculiar previously experienced sensations, but are therefore comprehensible
only to those who have known like experiences ; while
others echoing the deep chords which vibrate through all
humanity, are trumpet-calls to the peoples of the world.

What then are the higher and better kinds of art ?
Necessarily, those which awaken our higher, rather than
our lower and more sensual, emotions and feelings.
But the exercise and gratification of all our senses and
emotions, of our complete intelligence is good (I believe
no one will dispute so patent a truism if he realizes the
importance of the limitations which I put upon the
statement), provided this exercise and gratification is
the result of a legitimate cause and has legitimate

results. As Jean Jacques Rousseau has said, "Our passions are all good if we remain their master, all bad if we become subject to them." Therefore the greater the number of the complex factors which go to make up the nature of man, and it will be the better nature provided it is properly controlled in all its parts, the greater the number appealed to and touched, the broader must be the character of the work of art which touches them.

For example, a painting may tell a story and so, as already suggested, appeal to the literary, mental sense of the observer; or it may present charm of color and of form, and so awaken the æsthetic sense and delight the eye; again, it may strike a note which brings to the observer a new realization of the grandeur of nature, or the nobler qualities of man. Some compositions aim at and attain only one of these ends; others, greater in conception, are more wide reaching. Certain nude studies may be agreeable to the eye, but can go no farther. Jean Paul Laurens' fresco of St. Geneviève in the Pantheon at Paris tells a story, and is certainly not beautiful. On the other hand, turning to Raffaelle's "Madonna of the Chair" we find, combined in one small and simply painted canvas, beauty, a story, and a personification of motherhood. Thus the better works have many sides, appealing to corresponding sides in the nature of man. The manner in which these appeals are made is also varied.

It is probable that nearly all elements which we find beautiful (pleasing to a sense) are only so after our taste has been accustomed, educated to the partic-

ular sensation. We like olives or tomatoes only after
repeated trials. The first time a baby is given any
other food than milk, it spits out the distasteful substance. Some tastes however may be called natural
— they are perhaps the result of an unsullied environ-
ment, and are for our well-being, the fostering of life:
some may be called unnatural — they are like those
of opium, abortive, and destructive of life.[1] (It is not
necessary to enter here into the question of tastes which
have been overcultivated.) It is usually true that the
more healthful tastes are those which nature implants
in us: it therefore results that that kind of pleasant
sensation which is akin to the usual sensations she furnishes is liable to be the better. I believe we may
train ourselves into an admiration of the most peculiar
combinations of color, but that we should rather
educate our taste to delight, to the fullest extent, in
those subtilties which nature shows us continually in
her harmoniously toned out-of-doors.

It is probable too, that the interesting and the
moving are interesting or moving because we have
previously experienced similar sensations. This is
perhaps more definitely so in the former than in the
latter, because into the latter enters in greater degree,
an unknown quantity, instinct. It happens, here as
in the case of appeals to the senses only, that certain
topics of interest, certain moving episodes, hold their
power from broad, underlying, integral factors, in man's

[1] For a psychological discussion of this see Alfr. Lehman's "Die
Hauptgesetze des Menschlichen gefühlslebens," Leipsig, Reisland,
1892, pp. 294, etc., 195, 264.

life and nature; others are the result of artificial, unnecessary, and at times, undesirable conditions. And once more, what is natural is necessary and good; that which is unnatural is unnecessary and often bad. Hence it is better for a work of art to touch the beholder by recalling an episode, by reëchoing an emotion, of the more natural, *i.e.*, the higher kind. (It may be objected that altruism is not natural, but cultivated. That is not a question for us; as our present interpretation of "natural" is: "That which nature requires for the furtherance of her schemes for the progress of mankind"; therefore, that which is altruistic and ethical.)

These higher works, through the very conditions which govern their being, will be those which speak to men of different classes and countries, not because of the class or country, not because they are princes or paupers, classicists or decadents, Latin, German, or Anglo-Saxon; but because they are men. Instead of being approved by the initiated few and destined to die when the few are dead, they will, in time (a conventional symbol is more quickly recognized by the conventional than is the truth of nature), be acclaimed by the many, and shall live as the prophets of nature, so long as she herself lives.

A great work of art, then, must not only be able to influence a man through various channels; but must also be conceived so that it may influence different men. It must be all things to all men, as far as each individual is capable of response. We shall refer to this again when speaking of "Simplicity" in art.

It is natural that the man of the world who has passed his life in the midst of what is called cultured society (in a great measure a training school for the senses) should be the best judge of the beautiful in art, that the scholar should be the one to seek out the literary interest, the story of a composition; and that the man who has led a simple life, in touch with nature, should best recognize the genius, the soul in the artist's creation.

This is also true of the artist himself. What he lives, he will express. And to be a truly great artist one must aim at perfect technique and scholarliness; but keep in mind that these can never replace more simple, yet grander qualities that are the human, or rather the divine, elements in any branch of art.

CHAPTER II

INASMUCH as the expressions of the artist are the outcome of the nature and life of the man, in order to have a certain guide in choosing the best we must first investigate the great laws governing the character of art; laws, "which" as Ruskin puts it,[1] "based upon man's nature, not upon his knowledge, may possess so far the unchangeableness of the one, as that neither the increase nor imperfection of the other may be able to assault or invalidate them."[1] Describing these laws, the same author says in the following paragraph: "But more than this, exactly as we reduce to greater simplicity and surety any one group of these practical laws, we shall find them passing the mere condition of connection or analogy, and becoming the actual expression of some ultimate nerve or fiber of the mighty laws which govern the moral world. However mean or inconsiderable the act, there is something in the well doing of it which has fellowship with the noblest forms of manly virtue; and the truth, decision, and temperance, which we reverently regard as honorable conditions of the spiritual being have a representative or derivative influence over the works of the hand, the movements of the frame, and the action of the intellect."

Let us try to deduce and eliminate in the manner

---

[1] "Seven Lamps of Architecture."

suggested, laws which govern art in its highest expression; for while the greater part of the present volume must be taken up with technicalities, something should be said with regard to the character of art.

Foremost among the writers on this subject are two (one of them I have just quoted) whom I would urge every student to read. Tolstoi and Ruskin, though both noted for their erratic views and impossible to agree with in all of their technical deductions and applications, are still surely filled with the spirit and strike the keynote of that for which they plead so eloquently.

SINCERITY AND TRUTH

are the first great needs, or laws of art.

It is the revival of an old tale, this telling our artists to be truthful in their work; or rather, telling *would-be* artists to be truthful. Yet in spite of the different movements set on foot, and the intensity with which they have been pushed — perhaps because of this very intensity — we see imitations daily taking form around us. In our buildings, this is especially true; remembering that such effigies of architecture are signs of decadence, we may well feel uneasy.

If one of the geniuses of the twelfth century, one of those some of us are so ready to copy, had had the materials and methods of construction that we are granted, he would surely not have been at pains to hide or dress them up, merely that the result might seem like an admired, but constructionally inferior, preceding style. It is hard to imagine a Gothic architect building his pointed arch and filling it in with rubble and cement, in order to simulate the square heavy lintel of an Egyptian doorway; yet one has no difficulty in calling to mind examples of skeleton steel or wood construction, covered with terra cotta or whatnot, to masquerade as ogives or stone vaults.

Ruskin names three kinds of deceit in architecture: [1]

1. The suggestion of a mode of structure or support other than the true one.

2. The painting of surfaces to represent some other material than the real one.

3. The use of cast or machine-made ornaments of any kind.

The trickery of the first of these is usually quite apparent; for, either the imitation is badly done, or the designer is tempted to take advantage of possibilities, offered by the concealed construction, in a way that would be impossible with the real material. I have in mind a certain building whose long lintel, actually constructed of iron or steel, covered with terra cotta to imitate stone, would, if truthfully constructed, have forced the architect to recognize an ignorant and faulty intercolumniation by refusing to remain in place. But though a deception is not discovered, how much better to compose as pleasing a thing in a style the outcome of materials or circumstances present.

The application of this law to the steel skeleton office-building is revealed too infrequently. Indeed, some of our architects would seem to believe it quite

[1] "Seven Lamps of Architecture."

impossible to design a good-looking building whose walls do not appear to be of rusticated stone. And such men persist in their mania, even though the thinness of the reveals of the windows, as well as the actual height of the walls, make a use of the suggested material evidently impracticable.

What would have been done by a past age in such a dilemma? Is there no evidence of strong styles where the construction was made paramount, and frankly shown? Surely there are many examples. Gothic, for instance, is a continual reproach to us. But not to go so far back as the XII. and XIII. centuries, we find that the English, Flemish, German, and French architects of the Renaissance were able to construct apparent wood skeleton buildings, filled in with bricks and other materials, and were able to make the most beautiful kind of house, at that. Can we not do as well with protected steel beams covered with reënforced concrete or terra cotta that looks like what it is?

Of course nine tenths of the public of to-day would cry "Factory!" to such a suggestion. Yes, the buildings made of apparent iron beams and brick do look like factories and warehouses; but that is because the architect fails to bring any art to the help of the builder and engineer. I dare say, if the present day, this age of hurry and cheapness, had confided to it the fostering of a newly born style of wood construction, all attractive arrangements of beams, all carving of brackets, all art in the filling in of spaces, would be omitted, and again we might cry "Factory!"

The second of the heads suggested by Ruskin is exemplified in the chålets at Versailles, the Milan Cathedral, and in our own Colonial architecture. I shall never forget my pleasure in first seeing the charming little chålets in the gardens of the Petit Trianon. Hiding among the trees, they dotted the sunny park and its quiet lake and stream with reflecting and ever-changing colors, and peopled the landscape of my fancy with maids and gallants, half princely half peasant, flitting from house to dairy on their innocent errands. Nor shall I also forget my feeling of chagrined disillusion and disgust, on discovering the bricks and beams, even the ruined patches of these same chålets, to be all paint; a faithful picture of the purpose for which the whole was built, the poor sham of a rotten age!

The painted tracery and vaulting of Milan's Cathedral is so well known that it needs no comment; but it is well to keep in mind, as an example of the ill success of such artifices.

For our Colonial architecture, the architects of the time, at least, translated the proportions of Renaissance styles with which they were familiar, in such a way that the slender columns made no pretense of being other than painted wood. But our modern architects, having been to school just long enough to learn their orders (the proportions of stone construction), must need apply these with sagacious care, and lose all the charm of the older work.

With regard to the limits which should govern the introduction of architectural elements in painting, a suggestion of Ruskin's will suffice. He is referring to the ceiling of the Sistine Chapel, and remarks in his virile fashion: [1] "So great a painter as Michael Angelo would always stop short in such minor parts of his design, of the degree of vulgar force which would be necessary to induce the supposition of their reality; and strangely as it may sound, would never paint badly enough to deceive." That is the keynote of the whole question; a great artist would never deceive.

The third kind of deceit noted is the introduction of machine made ornament that purports to be hand made. The use of stamped and sanded galvanized iron to represent a carved cornice is well known in the cheap modern office and commercial building; this, be it said to their glory, American architects so much despise that one of our leading firms offered to pay, out of their own pockets, for a stone cornice, when a building committee would have contented themselves with a copper imitation.

There is another deceit that may be practiced in architecture, that is, with regard to the amount of work performed. Again an example will be sufficient explanation. Walking behind the balustrade in front of the François I. dormers in the Court at Blois, one notices the running decorations which surround these dormers to be discontinued, as soon as they are no longer visible from the ground. In such a case, if perfectly evident that there is waste of precious ornament on account of its being hidden, then no suggestion that the ornament continues should be allowed.

[1] "Seven Lamps of Architecture."

On the other hand, if there is a reason for making the suggestion, the ornament should be continued to the end.

This need of truth induces the need of character in a building, and brings us to the discussion of a second law.

CHARACTER

There are two kinds of character to be sought.

1. The work should bear the individuality of the artist.

2. The work should express that for which it has been constructed.

1. A work of art must show forth the individuality of the artist.

It is the personality of the artist which makes a work of art living; this we must realize when we remember that true art is the expression of a feeling, of an emotion which the artist has experienced.

There is a reassuring strain in the converse of such a truth, for while the expressed character of the artist is that which gives a creation vitality, he who is great enough to evolve an immortal composition is sure to have such strong characteristics and beliefs about art, that they force themselves into, and permeate, his work.

We have but to turn our eyes to the masterpieces of preceding ages to be convinced. No one would falter in placing the authorship of the "Night Watch," Botticelli's "Spring," or an hundred others. Who does not know a bit of Chopin the instant heard, or fails to recognize the difference in feeling between the balustrade of the tribune in the "Salle des Cariatides" in the Louvre, and the Jean Gonjou figures that support it?

I do not mean by this that an artist may not borrow from a preceding work of art, provided he imprints thereupon his personality.   Ruskin says,[1] "Now in the first place — and this is rather an important point — it is no sign of deadness in a present art that it borrows or imitates, but only if it borrows without paying interest, or if it imitates without choice." He speaks farther on of Raffaelle borrowing from Masaccio and Perugino. He might also have taken Shakespeare as an example to remind us how a genius may frankly adopt a plot and yet infuse into it new and greater spirit; or have told us how Gounod, yes, and the great Beethoven himself, have both used themes of Bach.

There is a point common to all these adaptations, of which we should not lose sight. The true artist never seeks to conceal what he has done, and to turn what has been an inspiration into plagiarism. Indeed he is usually too happy over his own interpretation of a motive not to insist on a recognition of the earlier one.

There is a flagrant error which should here be noted. It is the mistaking of the bizarre, of something merely different from what has been done before, for that which is personal.

I have found young students preferring one of two

[1] "Seven Lamps of Architecture."

architectural arrangements simply because some one
else had chosen the other; this despite the fact that
· that other would have been much the better. A man
of small nature who works for immediate fame is
likely to embrace, if he can not originate, the latest
fad, and become a decadent, a symbolist, or a neo-
impressionist. He has made a reputation as "that
clever artist who draws all his figures with a double
line," or "the man who catches the English girls so
dashingly," and so he continues paying more attention
to newspaper reports than to the sincerity of his work.

It was not so with Corot. Here we find an artist
heaped with abuse by the academicians of the age;
refused at the Salon, working quietly away at what
he feels and believes to be right, not because some one
is going to approve, not that he himself is going to
approve; but because he sees it thus, and loves the
portraying of it.

It should always be remembered that individuality
of expression can never be an excuse for faulty drawing, proportion, or composition. Indeed, no qualities can make up for such faults; while the sound worth
and sense of rest given by the opposite M. Henri
Mayeux aptly expresses in his treatise on decorative
composition.[1] "Cette manière libre de procéder, en
semant *au hasard* sur les formes des fleurs, des fruits,
des oiseaux ou des figures, sans tenir compte, le plus
souvent, ni de la courbure des surfaces, ni des arêtes
limitant les plans, accuse une absence de parti que ne

[1] Henri Mayeux, "La Composition Décorative," Librairies Imprimeries Réunies, Paris, pp. 73, 74.

saurait remplacer la facture la plus brillante. . . .
Si l'on supporte un décorateur du XVIIᵉ siècle lourd
et banal, grâce a la science avec laquelle il sait régler
ses compositions, on ne saurait admettre un artiste
japonais sans le diable au corps."

One of our great faults in America is the vast amount
of attention we pay to being original, to the detriment
of attaining actual worth and artistic strength. We
are continually crying out for a new style, or affecting
a borrowed one, instead of turning our attention to
serious technical study and allowing our personality
to assert itself. To quote again from Ruskin,[1] "A
day never passes without our hearing our English
architects called upon to be original and to invent a
new style; about as sensible and necessary an exhorta-
tion as to ask of a man who has never had rags enough
on his back to keep out cold, to invent a new mode of
cutting a coat. Give him a whole coat first, and let
him concern himself about the fashion of it afterwards.
We want no new style of architecture. Who wants
a new style of painting or sculpture? But we want
some style. It is of marvelously little importance if
we have a code of laws, and they be good laws, whether
they be new or old, foreign or native, Roman or Saxon
or Norman or English Laws. But it is of considerable importance that we should have a code of laws
of one kind or another, and that code accepted and enforced. . . . A man who has the gift will take up
any style that is going, the style of his day, and will
work in that and make everything that he does in it

[1] "Seven Lamps of Architecture."

look as fresh as if every thought of it had just come down from heaven. . . . Neither originality, therefore, nor change, good though both may be, and this is commonly a most merciful and enthusiastic supposition with respect to either, are ever to be sought in themselves, or can ever be healthily obtained by any struggle or rebellion against common laws. We want neither the one nor the other."

Perhaps the best way to close this discussion of individuality is to ask ourselves the question, "How can we make our work characteristic of us?" How? By doing as Corot did, executing what we really feel and love. Only that produced by an artist who takes pleasure in his creation will be good; in essence, that will always be good.

In one of the arches of the Cour Du Murier in the Ecole des Beaux Arts at Paris is a bronze figure, half finished, the fingers and other details merely blocked out. But a spirit of life pervades the bowed head, and draws one for a second look. Learning that the sculptor was only a student one wonders whence came the genius that could give so young a man such strength. Then the guardian tells of the passionate love the man had for his work; how one cold night, fearing the clay of the unfinished statue would freeze, he rose from his cot in a corner of the studio and wrapped his own coverings about the inanimate mass.

It is easy to guess the sequel, and know that we stand in the presence of the sculptor's spirit, itself shining from the eyes of the figure he died to save.

It would hardly do to ask all of our artists to die

c

for their work; there would be no more artists; but it is not too much to ask them to be willing to die for it. Loving our work, we will do it for its own sake, not for fame; still less on account of the money received; and we will never put up with a poor interpretation of it.

Ruskin [1] speaks of the attitude of our predecessors in architecture as being "the opposite of the prevalent feeling of modern times, which desires to produce the largest results at the least cost. We are none of us so good architects as to be able to work habitually beneath our strength; and yet there is not a building that I know of, lately raised, wherein it is not sufficiently evident that neither architect nor builder has done his best.

"It is the especial characteristic of modern work. All old work nearly has been hard work. It may be the hard work of children, of barbarians, of rustics; but it is always their utmost. Ours has as constantly, the look of money's worth; of a stopping short whenever and wherever we can; of a lazy compliance with low conditions; never of a fair putting forth of our strength."

A well-known Cleveland architect in speaking of the most respected architectural firm of the day said to me, "Their work, no matter what its faults, is always worth while and interesting on account of its workmanship. They never put up with bad stuff."

Ruskin's lecture on Turner [2] shows us a man of the type we should imitate. "There was another

[1] "Seven Lamps of Architecture."
[2] "Lectures on Architecture and Painting."

difference between Turner and other men. In doing these drawings for the commonest publications of the day, and for a remuneration altogether contemptible, he never did his work badly or because he thought it beneath him, or because he was ill-paid. There does not exist such a thing as a slovenly drawing by Turner.

"With what people were willing to give him for his work he was content; but he considered that work in relation to himself, not in its relation to the purchaser. He took a poor price that he might live; but he made noble drawings that he might learn. . . . He never let a drawing leave his hands without having made a step in advance, and having done better in it than he had ever done before; and there is no important drawing of the period which is not executed with a total disregard of time and price and which was not even then worth four or five times what Turner received for it."

Kipling has expressed in the "Envoi" of the Seven Seas the need of love for one's work, and we can hardly do better than turn to the testimony of a brother artist:

> " And only the Master shall praise us,
>   And only the Master shall blame;
>   And no one shall work for money,
>   And no one shall work for fame.
> But each for the joy of the working,
>   And each in his separate star,
> Shall draw the thing as he sees it
>   For the God of things as they are."

2. The work should express that for which it has been constructed.

Architectural compositions apparently range between two extremes; the useful and the ideal. If one looks into this carefully, one sees that it is really an expression of the laws just enounced.

As a first example: A factory is constructed for the manufacture of tin cans. Then the windows, the chimneys, each detail, should tend to further that end; a certain family look, common to such buildings, a certain character far more satisfactory than a costly, decorated façade, useless and out of harmony with the work done inside the walls, will be the result.

Here is another extract from the "Lectures on Architecture" which illustrates my point. "The first thing required of a building — not, observe, the highest thing — is that it shall answer its purpose, completely, permanently, and at the smallest expense. If it is a house, it should be just of the size convenient for its owner, containing exactly the kind and number of rooms that he wants with exactly the number of windows he wants, put in the places that he wants. If it is a church, it should be just large enough for its congregation, and of such shape and disposition as shall make them comfortable in it and let them hear well in it. If it be a public office it should be so disposed as is most convenient for the clerks in their daily avocations; and so on; all this being utterly irrespective of external appearance or æsthetic considerations of any kind, and all being done solidly, securely, and at the smallest necessary cost.

"The sacrifice of any of these first requirements to external appearance is a futility and absurdity.

Rooms must not be darkened to make the ranges of windows symmetrical. Useless wings must not be added on one side to balance useful wings on the other; but the house built with one wing if the owner has no need of two. . . ."

Never allow the hope of tickling the visual palate of the public, never let the better hope of beautifying our American cities, betray you into an architectural expression out of keeping with your program. In that case, you will have no more success than the spinster, whose young charms borrowed from the hair dresser and rouge pot do little to protect her from the sneers of kind friends.

But let us take another example. The building is to be a commemorative monument for a great man. Then let everything give way to such an expression. Here strength must be personified in massive supports; the details should be simple and scholarly, large in scale perhaps, forcing the beholder to realize that the house is that of a god rather than of a common mortal. The style must be in keeping with such a feeling; and the durability and undying power the old Egyptians knew so well how to compass, should, though interpreted in modern form, bear witness to the lasting fame and immortal soul, that crumbling stone is unable either to outlive or enclose.

The primary reason for a creation like that last described is an ideal one, and the so-called monumental feeling which forms such a large part — in the eyes of some men the only real part — of architecture, is an expression of this. In fact we may define the "monumental" as that which responds to the need of the ideal in contrast to that for merely human requirements.

G. Baldwin Brown, speaking of the ideal,[1] directs us to the prehistoric monuments of Western Europe, "these 'Menhirs' and 'Cromlechs' and 'Dolmens' of imperishable stone, often sublime by their very size and weight, and pregnant with a meaning which to us must ever remain obscure. . . . We can not gaze up at these rugged memorials of hoariest antiquity without feeling them to be the expression of some great idea that once filled the minds of their creators. What if this idea was immortality — that creed which formed the central point of the religion of Egypt —. . . ! We need not speculate upon this hazardous though fascinating theme; for all we want from these 'Rude Stone Monuments' is evidence that at a very early date in the history of humanity, men felt an impulse to embody the faith that was in them in some vast and enduring structure; a thing not for material use, but a witness to such spiritual conceptions as the family idea or the indestructibility of the human intelligence. So out of the performance of funeral rites — a family celebration and in a large sense of the word a festival — proceeds the desire for the permanent expression of the thought that filled every heart, and with the satisfaction of this desire, monumental architecture and not only this but monumental sculpture also are born." And farther on he says: "There is something megalithic, primeval, in the aspect of the noblest buildings of all times. . . . Give him an opportunity and

[1] G. Baldwin Brown, "The Fine Arts," Scribners, 1896, pp. 26–29.

allow him to create in freedom and every architect worthy of the name will build for an idea, will build massively and build forever, and a part not the least noble of this first of the arts will descend to it from the far-distant and unknown creators of Stonehenge and Carnac."

Once again, in discussing "Mass, Stability and Architectural Sublimity," [1] Mr. Brown suggests that the monumental feeling — the expression of something superhuman — may be obtained by an excess of the first two, as well as by the almost incredible labor evidenced in such a building as the Great Pyramid; or the wonderful intellectual strength and daring personified in the Forth Bridge, the Eiffel Tower or a Gothic Cathedral, all of which last he classes under the third head.

Later on, discussing "Scale," we shall see that it is not alone "Mass" that gives the monumental feeling. On the whole, it is better to keep to the broad definition, and remember that we shall succeed in inducing the "Monumental," by making our works for more than men; personifications of an idea. Thus did Michael Angelo, before us.

Most buildings of the present day have, in a measure, to satisfy demands of both the practical and the monumental. Although giving scope to the architect's imagination, this only complicates the problem. It is possible to triumph over the difficulties of such a situation by accentuating the peculiarities or characteristics of the special case.

[1] "Fine Arts," pp. 161–163.

All practically required elements should be frankly shown, never hidden through a fear of their not being decorative. This delineation of character can not be carried too far ; and in its finer expression it is one of the most difficult things to accomplish.

As a problem to demonstrate my meaning, I would suggest that five little sketches be made of commemorative monuments of the same dimensions, to express the very different programs following :

A monument to George Eliot.

A monument to Chaminade.

A monument to commemorate the founding of the French Republic.

A monument to commemorate the liberation of Cuba.

A monument in honor of Architecture.

The salt of each such monument, be it never so good, as a mere composition and piece of sculpture, will surely have lost its savor, if an inscription is needed to tell the tale.

FRANKNESS, DECISIVENESS

This is our third law.

One of the most distressing faults in a man is a vacillating temperament. A poor fellow who has not the strength of character to be good nor the wit to be really bad, a moral jelly-fish, awakes nothing but loathing. It is the story of the church of the Laodiceans, and we might well pray for another John the Divine to denounce anew, "I know thy works; that thou art neither cold nor hot. I would thou wert cold or hot.

So then because thou art lukewarm, and neither cold nor hot, I will spew thee out of my mouth. . . ."

Thus it is in art too.

First, to take the broadest sense : A composition that might have been done by any one, that might express anything, that might belong to any style, without positive faults merely because there is nothing to be faulty, is the poor, weak botch no one can tolerate.

Every one goes to see the Madeleine in Paris. Has any one ever had for it an enthusiastic word of praise ?

And this natural scorn of the undecided is the appropriate wage in all cases meted out by the final judge of art, Humanity, although the indecision be only in regard to details.

From the technical point of view the composition that is neither symmetrical nor unsymmetrical is bad ; those elements of a composition neither actually equal in value nor decidedly different are distressing. In short, anything "on the fence" is evidence, not only of want of training in the man who conceived the thought, but of the lack of a man, in the training which is supposed to have evolved an artist.

SIMPLICITY

Our fourth law, Simplicity, is needful for two reasons :

1. That the work of art may not contain details understood only by the initiated.

2. That the work of art may be readable ; *i.e.*, that the beholder may grasp the ensemble at the first glance, and so receive a strong impression.

1. In taking up the discussion of the first of these

two reasons, we may begin with the premise drawn
from an earlier page of this volume : Since the better
works of art, transmitting the nobler emotions, are
proved by their ability to reach men of all, of widely
differing, classes, many of whom are unacquainted
with the intricacies and complications of our modern
social machine, a truly broad, grand work of art can
not rely for success upon details understood only by
men of one class; but should be free from such details.

Tolstoi in his "What is Art?" [1] discusses this subject. He takes, as an example, the old Biblical tale
of "Joseph," calling it an example of universal art.
"That Joseph's brethren being jealous of his father's
affection sell him to the merchants; that Potiphar's
wife wishes to tempt the youth; that having attained
the highest station, he takes pity on his brothers, including Benjamin the favorite — these and all the rest
are feelings accessible alike to a Russian peasant, a
Chinese, an African, a child or an old man, educated
or uneducated; and it is all written with such restraint,
is so free from superfluous detail, that the story may be
told to any circle and will be equally comprehensible
and touching to any one." This he contrasts with
the modern novel, filled out, padded, in ways "which
make the stories difficult of comprehension to all
people not living within reach of the conditions described by the author. . . . The author of the novel
of Joseph did not need to describe in detail as would
be done nowadays, the blood-stained coat of Joseph,
the dwelling and dress of Jacob, the pose and attire of

[1] Count Leo Tolstoi, "What is Art?" Translation by A. Maude.

Potiphar's wife, and how, adjusting the bracelet on her left arm she said 'Come to me,' and so on, because the subject-matter of feelings in this novel is so strong that all details, except the most essential — such as that Joseph went out into another room to weep — are superfluous, and would only hinder the transmission of feelings. And therefore this novel is accessible to all men, touches people of all nations and classes, young and old, and has lasted to our times, and will yet last for thousands of years to come. But strip the best novels of our times of their details, and what will remain?"

Farther on he speaks of the difficulty of writing a simple poem, or of painting a simple picture, etc., "without any unnecessary details, yet so that it should transmit the feelings of the narrator; or to draw a pencil sketch which should touch or amuse the beholder; or to compose four bars of clear simple melody, without any accompaniment, which should convey an impression and be remembered by those who hear it."

He adds, in speaking of the final emancipation of art: "And therefore the ideal of excellence in the future will not be the exclusiveness of feeling accessible only to some, but, on the contrary, its universality. And not bulkiness, obscurity and complexity of form, as is now esteemed, but, on the contrary, brevity, clearness and simplicity of expression."

One of the most moving sketches I have ever seen was a small water color by Josef Israels. Done in practically two tones, it showed the bent figure of an old man resting on the brow of a hill silhouetted against the evening sky. Another picture of the same kind is Millet's shepherdess with the flock.

It is not difficult to see how the greatest artists have concentrated their attention on the real object of their masterpieces, leaving out all possible details; it seems still less difficult to turn from what they have done, and, forgetting their example, spend our time, if we be painters, painting buttons; architects, arranging cannon balls around the bases or cannon in the friezes of our commemorative monuments.

The architect who can only tell the story of his building or monument by the use of symbolical ornaments is but one step removed from the man who needs the all-powerful help of an inscription. Although the inscription is good in its place, still, character should be expressed by the feeling of the whole; by its sternness or its brilliancy; by the forbidding walls of the prison, or the rising shafts and lofty arches which carry our inspired thoughts to the Gates of Heaven.

2. That the work of art may be clear.

It is essential for force, indeed for any good impression, that a composition be easily grasped in ensemble.

The reason human beings enjoy anything is that they find in the enjoyment just the requisite amount of exercise of body or brain. Lehman [1] says of this: "Lust ist die psychische Folge davon, dass ein Organ während seiner Arbeit keine grössere Energiemenge verbraucht, als die Ernährungsthätigkeit ersetzen

---

[1] See Lehman's "Die Hauptgesetze des Menschlichen Gefühlslebens," Leipzig, Reisland, 1892, p. 156.

kann; unlust dagegen ist ein psychische Folge jedes Misverhältnisses zwischen Verbrauch und Ernährung, indem dieselbe entsteht, sowohl wenn der Verbrauch an Energie die Zufuhr überschreitet, als auch wenn die Zufuhr wegen Unthätigkeit des Organs das Maximum, das aufgenommen werden kann, überschreitet."

Quoting another writer:[1] "Mr. Herbert Spencer has given us a formula applicable to all these cases. For æsthetic pleasure, he explains, 'many elements of perceptive faculty must be called into play while none are overexerted; there must be a great body of the feeling arising from their moderate action, without the deduction of any pain from extreme action.'" Farther on, the same writer, speaking of clearness, says: "The physiology of the matter is evident. In a composition, say, of a picture, or of the façade of a building, if there is a medley of lines all running in different directions, the eye in following them is distracted and worried; it seeks to find a way through the maze, but is continually balked and turned aside. The same is the case if the lines all seem to lead away out of the composition in different directions; the eye then parts from the work and has each time to be brought back to it from the outside."

Whether or not the physiological or psychological theory just stated is sufficient to explain all kinds of æsthetic enjoyment, we must, at least, acknowledge the aptness of the example; and may pass to an investigation of how clearness is to be obtained.

Practically, we may direct our study from two

[1] G. Baldwin Brown, "Fine Arts," p. 191.

points of view as embodied in the two following statements :

(*a*) The interpretation of a compostion, the "facture," even though in itself pleasing, should not attract the attention.

(*b*) No minor subjects or details should exist which may make the principal emotion, subject, or motive, hard to find and grasp.

(*a*) If a writer is intent on expressing an idea which he wants others to receive, he does not choose a confused and distorted type for his book, interesting as the letters individually may be, nor does he use an obsolete or unusual form of language, however attractive or quaint; but he eliminates all distracting elements, so that the message he has to deliver may stand clearly forth.

I once asked a well-known painter his definition of an impressionist. "Why," he said, "all great painters are impressionists. Corot was an impressionist."

He was right; and, strange as it may sound, the impressionists are often not impressionists at all, much as they vaunt their allegiance.

One has but to look at a Corot to feel the early morning air of spring, to hear the light wind in the trees; and the graceful figure of a young girl but adds to the sensation, conveyed in the first glance, that here is both the fresh promise of life and a new day. How cheap, in contrast, are the fads of schools which distract the spectator from any appreciation of the subject, however strong in conception, by forcing upon his attention numberless spots of paint or a confusion of blocks.

In the rendering of an architectural drawing the

architect should see to it that, no matter how clever an effect may be obtained by "chic" contrasts, if the striking accompaniment to what is the real subject be out of keeping, or prevents a full appreciation of that subject, it should not be tolerated.

(b) In the same spirit, any impediment, through details, to a firm grasp of the dominating idea or motive of a composition should be ruthlessly swept away. The second part of the definition : "A masterpiece is that to which nothing can be added and *from which nothing can be taken*," must be kept carefully in mind.

Henri Mayeux,[1] in the "Composition Décorative," says of what he calls "la clarté" : ". . . c'est la vision façile et sans confusion, même à distance ; ce sont les motifs se lisant, quelle que soit leur complication, d'un seul coup d'œil et sans effort. L'indécision dans le parti adopté, l'abus des détails, le manque de franchise dans le rôle assigné à l'objet d'art, c'est-à dire tous les défauts opposés à la clarté, ne se retrouvent, hélas ! que trop souvent dans les productions courantes ; . . ."

Power is always gained by simplicity, and lost by the opposite ; yet the more intricate we make our compositions, the more are we tempted to congratulate ourselves for cleverness, and this with the open book of Nature at our side.

How grand is a stretch of sea with only a sand dune in the foreground ! As we stand gazing at the waves rolling in and breaking with ceaseless repetition on the beach, a bank of dark clouds moving towards us

[1] Henry Mayeux, "La Composition Décorative," p. 11.

from the horizon, no one of us fails to be impressed by the mighty spirit which envelops and bears us up, making us forget the finite, in the nearest approach our poor human preceptions can compass of the infinite. Truly, there are no details here to call us back from Heaven to Earth, from the contemplation of God's power to that of a carefully painted shell, standing obtrusively out from the picture.

We may be thankful that, though modern art seems at times to have lost her head, and to be playing with the butterflies and flowers by the wayside, Nature is always before us, a beacon light on the broad road to true greatness.

Yes! If we create strong, powerful works of art, we must adopt for our guidance the sibyl of simplicity.

CAREFULNESS; THOUGHTFULNESS

Farther back, under the heading of "Character," I said that an artist must love his work. Following the present plea for "simplicity," I want to add what may seem at first sight a negation of the former word, but which will prove, on consideration, the outcome of such love: "Do not waste your ornament."

I say that unwillingness to waste ornament should be the result of the artist's love for it. And is it not so?

The man who specifies a machine-made piece of "stock" is unconcerned as to whether it be plastered up in a place where it is useless or not. But the artist, who has spent himself on a bit of detail, is as unhappy at the thought of its desecration as is the mother whose child is carried away captive by barbarians.

Seeing wasted ornament, one realizes that it is cheap trash, cheaply disposed of.

There are three ways of wasting ornament: By making it of a kind unsuited to the material in which it is to be executed, by making it of a kind unsuited to what will be required of it, and by making it of a kind unsuited to the position it is to occupy.

To illustrate the first: Our American fashion of carving fine detail out of granite is the negation of art. If granite is the proper stone to use, a broader detail should be selected; or if the fine work is in character, a more delicate stone should be chosen.

Ruskin speaks of this and of the second manner of waste, as follows:[1] "Finally, work may be wasted by being too good for its material or too fine to bear exposure; and this, generally a characteristic of late (Gothic), especially of Renaissance work, is perhaps the worst fault of all. I do not know anything more painful or pitiful than the kind of ivory carving with which the Certosa of Pavia, and part of the Colleone Sepulchral Chapel at Bergamo, and other such buildings are incrusted. . . . And this is not from the quantity of it, nor because it is bad work — much of it is inventive and able; but because it looks as if it were only fit to be put in inlaid cabinets and velveted caskets, and as if it could not bear one drifting shower or gnawing frost. We are afraid for it, anxious about it and tormented by it; and we feel that a massy shaft and a bold shadow would be worth it all."

The third way of wasting ornament — misplacing it

[1] "Seven Lamps of Architecture."

D

— has been already referred to, on account of the false suggestions which may result. Either ornament should be suited to the place it is to occupy, or the place should be suited to the ornament.

No work, even in detail, should ever be slighted. An ornament which is blocked out bears the same relation to a finely cut piece that indication does to detailed drawing. Indication does not consist of putting all the lines in quickly and, consequently, anywhere; but, instead, of carefully selecting the characteristic lines, and, while making such a selection as limited as possible, of putting them in exactly the proper places.

To quote again from Ruskin on this subject:[1] "In the modern system of architecture decoration is immoderately expensive, because it is wrongly placed and wrongly finished. I say first wrongly placed. Modern architects decorate the tops of their buildings. Mediæval ones decorated the bottom. That makes all the difference between seeing the ornament and not seeing it. If you bought some pictures to decorate such a room as this, where would you put them? On a level with the eye, I suppose, or nearly so? Not on a level with the chandelier? . . .

"Not that the Greeks threw their work away as we do. As far as I know Greek buildings their ornamentation, though often bad, is always bold enough and large enough to be visible in its place. It is not putting ornament high that is wrong, but it is cutting it too fine to be seen wherever it is. . . .

[1] "Lectures on Architecture and Painting," John Wiley and Sons, New York, 1890, pp. 59 and 61. Also addenda, pp. 104 and 106.

"However, as this great Gothic principle seems yet unacknowledged, let me state it here, once for all, namely, that the whole building is decorated, in all pure and fine examples, with the most exactly studied respect to the powers of the eye; the richest and most delicate sculpture being put on the walls of the porches or on the façade of the building, just high enough above the ground to secure it from accidental (not from wanton) injury. The decoration as it rises becomes *always* bolder, and in the buildings of the greatest times, *generally* simpler. . . .

"The façade of Wells Cathedral seems to be an exception to the general rule, in having its principal decoration at the top, but it is on a scale of perfect power and effectiveness; while in the base modern Gothic of Milan Cathedral the statues are cut delicately everywhere, and the builders think it a merit that the visitor must climb to the roof before he can see them; and our modern Greek and Italian architecture reaches the utmost pitch of absurdity by placing its fine work *at the top only*."

In order that an architect may properly understand the application of his ornament, he should be, in some degree at least, both painter and sculptor. This the truly great architects of the past have been: Phidias Giotto, Michael Angelo, Jean Goujon, and how many others! The genius that directed the best of what was done in the architecture of the French Renaissance also guided the hand that carved the charming figures of the Fontaine des Innocents.

The round ball, or "Dutch cheese," which one sees,

from time to time, perched with consummate grace on the top of a gate post, bearing testimony to the quality of the inventive genius of a poor architect who can imagine nothing more interesting, is an apt example of what the following decries:[1] "Being, as I have said, in reality not architects but builders, they can indeed raise a large building, with copied ornaments, which, being huge and white, they hope the public may pronounce 'handsome.' But they cannot design a cluster of oak-leaves — no, nor a single human figure — no, nor so much as a beast or a bird, or a bird's nest! Let them first learn to invent as much as will fill a quatrefoil, or point a pinnacle, and then it will be time enough to reason with them on the principles of the sublime."

And now, a few practical suggestions to give us courage, for the reader will say that it is not worth while trying to be an architect if it is necessary to be all else first.

Not each one of us, it is true, has the artistic spirit in the same degree; but if we are glad to do what we are doing, an early inability to do it well should not disturb us. Some artists, often the greatest, develop but slowly; and the truly artistic nature, in its embryonic stage, is evidenced more by the love of art, coupled with innate delicacy of temperament, refinement, and strength of character, than by the clever brush or pencil stroke we are tempted to accept as its index.

Guilbert, one of the strongest decorators the Ecole des Beaux Arts can boast, began as a poor, an impos-

---

[1] "Lectures on Architecture and Painting," p. 180.

sible "nouveau," a youth pitied by his comrades. I remember a retrospective exhibition of Israels' work in The Hague, where the early canvases were the most abominable daubs ever hung before the public. On inquiry, it appeared that the great painter did not find himself until he was over thirty years old. Evidences of a like inability are to be seen in early examples of Corot's work in the Mesdag collection in The Hague.

Let us take up, in succession, the important points which an architect has to keep in mind.

First of all, he must reason. As our professor used to tell us at the studio (it was, I believe, an old quotation from the "atelier André"): "Le raisonnement; c'est la base de l'Architecture."

Reason about the character of the building you intend to construct. Reason about your choice of a certain scheme of composition. Reason in your choice of motives. To sum it all up, follow the general advice given to the young chess player: "Never make a move without having a reason for it."

Second, he must cultivate the imagination in every possible way. He should form the habit of allowing one impression, or sensation, to suggest another; and with this, try to cultivate a power of remembering what has been observed.

After having seen a building, try to recall the different elements and details distinctly enough to reproduce them. Power of memory may be fostered by use in the most unimportant affairs; at a reception, for instance, business should be allied to pleasure, in noting new gowns and describing them after a return home.

In the use of impressions or ideas, keep well in mind that an ornament of one sort may form the motive of a decoration of one entirely different. A Norwegian necklace may be the bud from which is to flower forth a frieze, or the belt at the base of a dome. No bit of decoration is insignificant enough to be ignored. Fill the mind with motives; so full that there will be no danger of being induced to copy any one motive. Study everything that has been done; thus you may learn to avoid what is bad, while assimilating what is good.

An excellent manner of studying is to take up different styles successively, making several compositions in each.

Third, the architect should draw continually, that he may become master of his pencil.

M. Henri Deglane once voiced this rule for acquiring a good "touch": "Carry a two sous sketch-book with you, and draw everything you come across with a soft (a, B. B.) pencil, using the fewest possible lines." He might have added: "and never pressing hard on the paper."

Last of all, the great teacher of artists, to whom all return sooner or later, is Nature; and be he painter, sculptor, or architect, the student, yes, and the master, can find no more beautiful harmony of color than is shown in the soft violet and gray tones of autumn and winter hillsides; or in the glories of the fiery sunset; and he will always fall short, in his creations, of the wonderful contrasts of line and form which the human body, his own servant, displayed during unconscious babyhood.

PART II

CHAPTER I

THE PRINCIPLES OF COMPOSITION

WE have discussed the general laws of character governing an artistic composition; let us now turn to the technical laws that will aid us in obtaining an effect. Thus we may work knowingly, masters of our subject; and not merely from sentiment, putting together, in a heterogeneous mass, what seems to us, for the moment, pleasing.

And first of all, a word with regard to the nature of these principles would not be amiss.

I do not believe that there is a fixed standard of beauty of proportion; or, for that matter, of shape, or color, sound, or taste.

For example, the Egyptians considered beautiful a certain type of face, which we, nowadays, find merely bizarre. We moderns, it is true, have seen the Greek face so often portrayed that we have come to admire it; but would a Greek, think you, tolerate the fin-de-siècle brunette of a Paris salon, or even some of the "Gibson girls" we thought attractive at one period?

Then as regards the proportion of the human figure — few men of to-day would be enthusiastic over a

39

woman whose dainty head was but a seventh or eighth of her total height.

As with our ideas of correct proportion in the human form, so with architectural forms.

For several hundred years, certain proportions were held proper for the columns of the temples of Egypt. Then the inhabitants of another country, Greece, became used to quite another proportion; and finally the "classic" column was evolved, and made imperative, by the Roman builders. So on through the Middle Ages, changes of fashion. altered the current idea of what was beautiful; until, after the French Renaissance had contented itself with the most unclassic proportions, we are come back again to the rule of the Romans.

But this is only true of mere comparative dimensions, etc. With the laws of composition it is quite another thing; for they, like the laws already discussed, are derived from human characteristics. The fact that man's mind tires quickly of monotony would induce us to decorate a certain portion of our composition, leaving the rest bare. Thus would we satisfy the human demand of "contrast."

First let us agree upon the definition of the word "composition," calling it, if you will, the art of forming a whole, by uniting different parts.

According to Webster, from the point of view of the fine arts, it is "The art, or practice, of so combining the different parts of a work of art as to produce a harmonious whole." G. Baldwin Brown in "The Fine Arts" says:[1] "It is the first essential in

---

[1] G. Baldwin Brown, "The Fine Arts," Scribner, 1896, p. 114.

a work of art that it should present itself as a unity, and not a mere formless mass of indefinite extension." Thus the cornice of an elevation, like the cadence in music, is an element which crowns or limits the work. Moreover, in a composition, since the different parts must unite, harmonize, there must be no inharmonious or foreign elements.

There may be uninteresting compositions that contain no inharmonious elements, and this because of monotony in the arrangement, or as a result of the whole composition being of equal or like interest.

That a composition may be interesting, then, it must always contain unlike points of interest.

But if these different points of interest, or focal points, attract the attention equally, there will again result a diffusion of the perceptions of the observer.   Therefore there must be a studied gradation in the different points of interest; and, recurring to our definition — they, in turn, must harmonize or unite with each other.

Last of all, if there is to be a gradation in the amount of interest the different points possess, there will inevitably be a principal point of interest.

To enounce all of this in definitely stated laws: In a composition,

1. *The interest must be focalized, and have its most potent expression in one point.* (This point we shall call the climax.)

2. *The number of secondary focal points must be reduced to minimum; where such points exist they must be conceived primarily in regard to the climax and in their comparative importance must work up to it.*

3. *Of the different minor elements of the composition each, perhaps, relating to its own especial focal point, must still feel the influence of the climax.*

4. *In a pictorial composition the different elements must balance in such a manner that the average of interest will fall in the middle of the frame. In the other visual arts, balance in relation to the center of gravity must be observed.*

5. *That the different elements of a composition, climax, secondary climaxes, and submotives, may attain to the highest interest, they must contrast one with the other.*

6. *That unity exist in the composition, the laws of harmony must be observed, and no foreign element introduced.*

The general result of the first of these laws is, evidently, that:

(a) The climax must be the most interesting motive of the composition.

For example, one would avoid placing an unimportant diamond-pointed block in a surrounding circle of cupids; if there is a difference of material, the principal motive should be of the more precious; if there are differences of projection, the principal motive should have the most pronounced one; if there are differences of color, the most striking should be for the climax, and so on.

(b) The climax must have the most important position.

In a composition which is to be appreciated in sequence, this position is at the end; as, for instance, in a drama, an opera, or a succession of pictures. How our perceptions are sated by the repetition, in like degree, of a sensation, is too well known — we are too familiar with the trick of taking a pinch of salt after pudding, in order that we may find sweetness in an orange — to make a long discussion of this statement necessary.

In a composition to be apprehended by a single glance, the principal motive should be placed where the eye will most readily find it, not too near the edge of the composition. If the climax is near the edge of the composition, the preponderance of interest there will become so great that it will be difficult to carry out the fourth law. A picture or a building would enter the category of works of art to be seen in a single glance. The statue is an admissible exception (as many designs where silhouette is of great importance, the crowning climax being approached in sequence), because we are so used to looking to the head for the chief expression as to experience no difficulty in finding it there.

The first law (also the second and third) is subject to the fifth and sixth laws, of "Contrast" and "Unity." An interesting piece of decoration is most striking surrounded by a blank wall, and must be of the same family as the rest of the composition.

The need of a close observance of the second law is evident, since each secondary focal point necessarily detracts somewhat from the importance of the climax. In a small composition, these secondary points may be entirely eliminated. As to the interrelation of the climax and lesser elements, Lehman,[1] quoting Fechner's

[1] "Die Hauptgesetze des Menschlichen Gefühlslebens," pp. 207 and 210.

"Prinzip der ästhetischen Folge"[1] and "Prinzip der ästhetischen Versöhnung,"[2] states the two following laws: "Wenn zwei oder mehr entweder lust- oder unlustbetonte, gleichartige Vorstellungen, die nur in betreff der Stärke ihrer Gefühlstöne verschieden sind, aufeinander folgen, so wird die resultierende Summe der Lust oder Unlust verschieden werden, je nachdem schwächere Lust oder Unlust einer stärkeren vorausgeht oder umgekehrt. Und näher bestimmt wird der Unterschied der Gefühlssumme der, dass die möglichst grosse Lust oder die möglichst geringe Unlust, die unter den gegebenen Umständen zu erreichen ist, durch eine Bewegung in positiver Richtung, d. h. von der stärkeren zur schwächeren Unlust oder von der schwächeren zur stärkeren Lust, entsteht; umgekehrt wird die wenigste Lust oder die grösste Unlust durch eine Bewegung in negativer Richtung entstehen, eine Bewegung also von der stärkeren Lust zur schwächeren, von der schwächeren Unlust zur stärkeren." "Das Versöhnungsgesetz: Wenn zwei oder mehr teils lust- teils unlustbetonte gleichartige Vorstellungen, nur hinsichtlich der Stärke ihrer Gefühlstöne verschieden aufeinander folgen, so wird die nach den Umständen möglichst grosse Lust oder möglichst geringe Unlust dadurch erreicht werden, dass die Bewegung als Totalität in positiver Richtung geht, und die möglichst geringe Lust oder die möglichst grosse Unlust entsteht, wenn die Bewegung als Totalität in negativer Richtung geht."
Thus the first of these laws tell us that where the

[1] "Vorschule der Aesthetik," II., p. 234.
[2] Ibid., II., p. 238.

elements are either all pleasant or unpleasant in order
to obtain the greatest enjoyment or the least distress
each element must be more pleasing or less displeasing
than its predecessor in suite. Explaining the second
of the laws,[1] Lehman gives the example of a suite of
unpleasant sensations and one pleasant sensation.
To obtain the greatest delight, the unpleasant sensations must precede the pleasant one. The suite of
unpleasant sensations may, however, progress from
the most unpleasant to the least so, finally reaching the
climax in the pleasant ending; or it may progress from
the least unpleasant to the most so, what is thus lost
being made up for by the intensified contrast when
the pleasant sensation is brought in. Lehman says
either method gives about the same degree of pleasure
in the end.

The reasons for the second clause of the second
law, and for the third law are obvious. Every effort
must be made to give importance to the principal
motive. In other words, in a strong composition, one
of the chief missions of the secondary motives is to
make compensation for their existence, by absolute con-
formity to the characteristics evinced in the climax.

From the point of view of form, two lines compose
one with the other when the first leads into, and continues; or when the first is perpendicular to the second.
In this latter case the lines also give contrast.

Balance is a popular word; yet our fourth law is
often violated where one would least expect to find it
so. If one does not wish to feel that a pictorial sub-

[1] "Die Hauptgesetze des Menschlichen Gefühlslebens," p. 211.

ject has been badly placed in its frame, where a weight of interest exists on the right, or above, a balancing weight of interest must be placed on the left, or below. Between two such masses, if one is more concentrated and powerful than the other, the stronger is kept farther from the edge of the composition.

The need of contrasts in the elements of a composition results from the fatigue which the human mind sustains in a monotonous repetition, and in the desire it has for the excitement of change. Moreover, contrasts intensify the effect of the motives that produce them.

How distressing is the even repetition of notes, by means of which an ardent student of music in the next apartment is driving you to distraction. How uninteresting, by itself, would be the recitative of an opera, which, however, in the composition you welcome as a relief after a moving solo or duet?

The single principal motive will show, in contrast to a series; in line, one line is brought out by being made perpendicular to its fellow; a wide space is intensified by an accompanying narrow one; a dark space is given interest by a light one next; one color shows forth, a striking contrast to its complement.

The sixth law of Unity embraces four distinct and very important heads, which we may call, as follows, the laws of harmony, viz.: Character, Style, Color, and Scale.

(a) UNITY OF CHARACTER

In the general discussion of character it was determined a building must express both the personality of the artist and the use for which created. It seems almost superfluous to add what is so evident, that each part of the building should express the same thing; yet herein is an error often committed.

An artist may begin the composition of his building with the firm intention of carrying out a certain impressive feeling, but later on, becoming interested in a detail, he evolves a motive entirely out of keeping with the rest of his design. It often happens, too, that different parts of a composition are for unlike uses, and must, despite the fact that they belong to the same ensemble, show distinct individuality. The Art Building and Machinery Hall of a World's Fair would exemplify this. Here unity would be attained by making all the buildings of the fair in keeping with the idea of the progress of the world and illustrative of the temporariness of that to be used for only a limited space of time.

(b) UNITY OF STYLE

Style is the imprint a particular epoch makes on art.

If, then, the elements of one style are introduced in the expression of a different one, evidently discord will result. We might call this a fault of character, for such an element bears the mark of the characteristics of its age, entirely foreign to that of another age. Thus an Egyptian column in a Renaissance ballroom, or a Renaissance motive in a Gothic church, will always be as oil and water to each other.

I do not mean by this that an architect may not unite in the same composition motives inspired from different styles, provided he does it logically. The artist will then stamp each element with his own modern personality, so that, although the ideas of form have been suggested by unlike archæological examples, the final results, all showing the feeling of the present time, will actually be of the same style, a modern one. This is the application which we may make of a study of style. As Henri Mayeux says:[1] "Le style, que l'on confond souvent avec le caractère, est le cachet, la marque spéciale des œuvres d'un pays ou d'une époque: chercher à faire revivre celui d'un siècle passé, c'est nécessairement le déflorer; on n'est plus dans les conditions voulues de temps et de milieu, et de l'imitation on ne tarde pas à tomber dans la pastiche. L'étude des styles, excellente pour l'éducation de l'artiste qui s'instruit en comparant, ne peut servir, si on s'avise de lui demander davantage, qu'à étouffer dans leur germe tout art et tout originalité."

(c) Unity of Color

This is a need, though commonly felt, most difficult of analysis. There must be no discord in the combination of colors used. And yet, what rule is there by which the discord may be avoided, the unity retained?

A musician will hand you a work on "harmony" where you may find catalogued all the possible faults, and see the agreeable sequences set forth; you may carry this book to a physicist, who will analyze each rule and tell you "why."

[1] Henri Mayeux, "La Composition Décorative," p. 176.

But no physicist has yet informed us why most forms of red and blue will not harmonize, except by the vague, negative announcement that "complementary colors go together." (Pure red and blue are not complementary.) The whole must really be a subtle expression of the artist himself.

We may make a few deductions from nature; and after suggesting these, with a word of warning about complementary colors, leave the subject.

It is a recognized fact that all colors harmonize out of doors, provided they are at a distance, or have the sun on them. In each case the reason is a like one; at a distance, the atmosphere creates a tone which mingles with the different colors, bringing them together; in the sunlight, the brilliant warm rays (they are warm or pinkish, probably, from the refraction of the atmosphere, an accentuation of this being observable at sunset or sunrise) make a similar tone, which enters into the composition of all local color. In the case of the sunlight, it may be possible that the eye is made less perceptive of differences in color by the brilliancy of the light and the afterimages created.

This suggests a first rule: any number of colors will harmonize, provided each has in its composition a common one, which may be called the tone.[1] The tone, if pure and brilliant, must not overpower the

---

[1] What is meant here is the combination of the effect of a tone-pigment with that of other pigments representing local color. The result must be that given by the blending of the colors on a rotating wheel; as when two pigments are *very* thoroughly mixed, before application, the mixture does not give the effect of the union of unmixed color.

E

local color, or assert itself as such; and if gray, must not make the local color "dirty."

It has long been known that two complementary colors harmonize. They do so in one of two ways: If both are pure and brilliant, the result will be garish, barbaric. If one is dull and dark, the other pure and brilliant, the combination will be more subtle, and to the modern taste, more agreeable.

In general, three or more colors which combine together (when being rotated on a wheel) and form white in certain proportions, will, in the same proportions, be agreeable in juxtaposition.

Lastly, any colors broken up in small enough spaces (as a mosaic) to form, in a measure, a tone will be agreeable, provided the tone is not itself dirty, or disagreeable.

Practically, the way to avoid discords in designing is to come back, fresh, to a study that has been put aside, and eliminate any dissonant note the first glance detects.

(d) UNITY OF SCALE

In the visible arts, "scale" is that aspect of a motive which, irrespective of the actual size of the motive, suggests dimensions for it.[1]

Our impression of scale in a motive comes from seeing certain elements always made (for logical reason or

---

[1] The term "scale," when used in this sense, is entirely different in meaning from the like word (which I shall call "numerical scale") in such a sentence as: "The scale of $\frac{1}{8}$ of an inch to the foot." The latter is merely the name of a comparative measure.

custom) of definitely appointed sizes. Thus, seeing the drawing of such an element, and having in mind its real dimensions, we form an idea of the proportion that exists between the drawing and nature; in other words, receive an impression of the numerical scale (one eighth, one fourth or one half an inch to the foot) at which the drawing is made. Also, especially after one has become used to working at any of these numerical scales, through appreciating that a certain known object in nature is of a relative known size in a drawing, from the size of another new object in the same drawing, one may form a correct idea of the real size of the latter in nature.

Appreciating this, we may formulate the two conditions on which is based unity of scale.

I. In a drawing the different elements should all seem to be depicted at the same numerical scale.

II. The general aspect of scale (not numerical scale) of the composition should be in accord with nature; or, taking into consideration the numerical scale of a drawing, the design once executed should be in accord with nature.

A motive, or the drawing of a motive, complying with these laws is said to be "in good scale" or "good in scale."

A *drawing* is "small in scale" when it seems to be shown at a smaller numerical scale than the one used (one eighth perhaps instead of one fourth of an inch to the foot). The realization of such a drawing would have smaller actual dimensions than those suggested, or inversely, from the delineation of a motive that is small in scale one would be led to expect a much larger realization than the actual one.

A *motive* is "small in scale" when its elements are smaller than they should be; when it looks the diminished counterpart of an object of the normal world; when it seems created for the use of dwarfs or dolls, rather than men.

To make a drawing or motive small in scale is the most distressing manner of transgressing the laws of scale. It implies an effeminate temperament in the finished artist, and must be guarded against by the student. In his early studies he will be tempted to smallness by an almost universally experienced tendency to overmultiply the number of elements in his compositions.

A *drawing* is "large" or "big in scale" when it seems to be shown at a larger numerical scale than the one to which it is actually drawn. The realization of such a drawing would have larger actual dimensions than those suggested.

A *motive* is large in scale when it seems to be constructed for beings of a greater stature than that of man.

The fault of bigness of scale is less unfortunate than that of smallness of scale. It implies a certain robustness of temperament, a male strength of character in the artist that we unconsciously admire; and, provided the relation between nature and the composition can be established, the actual dimensions of the building, let us say, made apparent, the beholder is impressed with a sense of awe, feeling himself before a building made for something more than puny human needs.

A composition large in scale takes precedence over surrounding or accompanying compositions, and acquires the characteristics which we denominate as monumental (see pages 21 and 22). In an exhibition of drawings, the one slightly larger in scale than those about, other things being equal, will make a better impression, and in any case "carry" better than its fellows.

The dangers of bigness of scale are twofold: it is often difficult to make evident the relation nature bears to the composition, and there usually results grossness and want of refinement in the design. The first of these errors is noticeable in the interior of St. Peter's of Rome; it takes the beholder half an hour to realize the enormous size of the monument, and as a result he never experiences the full impression which should be his. An example of the second fault is furnished, to some extent, by the detail of the Paris Opera House, a masterpiece whose wonderful qualities of brilliancy and strong composition make us regret all the more poignantly a certain suggestion of heavy and vulgar display.

An impression of largeness of scale may be actually sought for a tomb or other similar composition, the requirement being that the comparative scale of nature be made evident.

That an object "has no scale" implies there is no means of determining from its aspect the relative scale of nature. This is most faulty in a complete composition, although a few elements usually having no scale (such as the classic column) are of so established a use that they have become admissible.

REQUIREMENTS OF GOOD SCALE [1]

There are four requirements to be observed in order that good scale may be retained : (1) the requirement of human needs ; (2) the requirement of material elements ; (3) the requirement of natural relative proportion ; (4) the requirement of the visual distance as governed by the ensemble.

1. *The Requirement of Human Needs*

Nearly all objects have a distinct relation to our physical wants, and, such a relation existing, must be carefully respected. A step is cut for the practical purpose of making an ascent easy; therefore the proper height of the step is that the average man finds most convenient. Thus a certain unchangeable unit, independent of the scheme of decoration, is established.

Other examples of this are : the height of a balustrade ; the height of a table ; of a desk ; of bookcases ; the size of a bed ; the spacing of bars in a grille or grating, etc. It results that in a composition such elements may express and establish the actual size of the whole design. The two doors with their flights of steps (Fig. 1) will illustrate this from the architectural point of view, while a less architectural example

---

[1] See also Mayeux, " La Composition Décorative," pp. 106 to 125. M. Mayeux makes a division which I have not followed exactly, but the general suggestions are practically the same.

is given by the contrast between the two bells shown (Fig. 2).

FIG. 1.

From this principle we may deduce a method of testing the scale of an architectural composition. First,

FIG. 2.

taking only into consideration the general aspect of the design, let us draw a man, making him as tall, in relation to the building or monument, as seems proper. Then, let us measure his height: if six feet, we may feel satisfied that our building is in good scale; if ten or twelve feet, we know the composition is too big in scale and must re-study; if the figure proves but three or four feet high, we must confess our monument small in scale, and should best rub it out and begin anew.

Moreover, on drawing out, at its proper size, an element which has a practical use, if we imagine it too large in proportion to the rest of the composition — if what we have just drawn in proper scale seems out of scale — we are thereby informed that, in reality, the whole design is small in scale.

2. *The Requirement of Material Elements*

(*a*) The dimensions of materials may determine the size of a composition in which the materials appear. Some of these dimensions are absolute; some derived from custom. Thus the size of slate in a roof is derived from material limitations; bricks, tiles, etc., are usually made of a certain size because of practical considerations, while the arbitrary height of the courses, fifteen or sixteen inches in rusticated stonework, is often so remotely connected with actual dimensions necessity prescribes that we must admit the requirement, though irrefragable, to be one of custom.[1]

(*b*) The requirements of construction may also de-

[1] I am here referring to the regular rustications of later Renaissance and modern work; not, of course, to the Florentine or Romanesque work, etc., or to the styles derived therefrom.

termine the size of a motive, or at least suggest relative sizes for motives of unlike construction. A stone
arcade may have three points of support to one of the

FIG. 3.

steel and glass marquise before it (Fig. 3) ; a large bay
will be closed by a fixed frame, while one of lesser di-

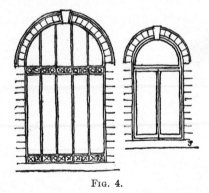

FIG. 4.

mensions may be an ordinary casement window
(Fig. 4). A very usual stumblingblock to the beginner

is the comparison of scale that exists between different forms of bays.

It is a fact that in the same composition bays constructed of the same material, but of different forms, should, in order that unity of scale may be preserved, have correspondingly different spans. There is a nice balancing of two principles, which probably furnishes the reason for this. We know that a flat arch will span a greater distance than a lintel can, and a semicircular arch a still greater distance. Moreover, the thrust of a flat arch makes it less appropriate for a wide span than a semicircular arch would be. As a result of this, we are accustomed to see semicircular arches used to cover great distances, and therefore feel that they have more scale than flat arches or lintels (Fig. 5).

But, *a fortiori*, it might be urged that the pointed

Fig. 5.

arch, giving less thrust than the semicircular, or segmental arch, must have the greatest scale; whereas this is not the case.

When we remember that the thrust of an arch may not be the only requirement limiting its application, but that its adaptability must also be taken into consideration, we shall understand this. Given the form of an arch, the span, unluckily, governs the rise, so that, for very wide spans, the pointed arch, necessitating too great height, becomes impossible. And so, within certain limits laid down by the aforesaid balance of these considerations, the broader of two semicircular arches (as in Fig. 5) will usually have the greater scale.

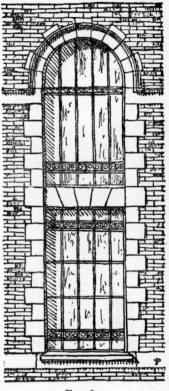

Care must be taken whenever a comparison between a square and circular opening occurs, that the circular opening be the wider.

A Palladian motive whose square bays are too nearly equal to the circular one is most distressing, and the common use of this motive, in our modern Colonial architecture, where the central circular opening is no wider than square-headed windows in other parts of the design, is decidedly faulty.

Fig. 6.

An apparent exception to the above rules is the circular opening placed over a square one of the same width. Here, however, the sides of the upper windows should carry down to the lower, making in reality only one bay (Fig. 6).

As a last caution, it is unwise to make an arch within an intercolumniation where the columns project much from the wall. Such a combination is only good when the entablature of the colonnade is evidently one with the

FIG. 7.

wall of the arcade, showing that, although it may have a flat arch construction of its own, it also derives support from the circular arch below. If the two elements seem independent of each other, the wide square opening will appear out of scale with the narrow arched one (Fig. 7).

3. *The Requirement of Natural Relative Proportion*

In an element, or in similar elements of a composition, that unity of scale may be retained, figures, animals, flowers, plants, instruments and other decorative objects, must be depicted in their natural relative sizes.

In other words, a terrified damsel must not be shown fearfully contemplating her instant death at the paws of a toy lion. If there is not space in a composition to introduce a second, full-sized human figure, a baby, rather than a reduced man, should be shown.

It is well to preserve the same numerical unit of scale in all elements of one design; but, under certain conditions, the opposite of this is true. There are even exceptions, where single elements must have details of individual scale.

We shall take up the several cases successively.

There may be a difference in the general numerical scales of two or more elements of the same composition, provided: (a) the elements are unlike in essence, and are in separate compartments or divisions — the central motive of a tapestry, or painting, might have an entirely different unit of scale from the border; or, again, the scale of the vertical supports of a piece of furniture may not be the same as that of the panels or doors between them; while the decoration of the shaft of a column would be different in scale from that of the wall in the intercolumniation; (b) the elements have a different expression — one is a bas-relief, while the other is in decided projection, or one is monochrome, the other in color; (c) the elements are of different materials — the bronze handles and stand of a vase might be at another scale than the faïence, or a bit of carved ivory different from the wood carving next to it; (d) one of the elements is conventionalized, while the other is not, as in the central motive of a tapestry or decoration, where a subject, represented in a natural manner, may be surrounded by a conventional design (see Fig. 33, *e*); also busts, termini, masks, lions or goats' heads, chimères, finials, rosettes, etc., as accessories, would come under this head. But in all of these cases a certain condition must be observed, viz.: as the scale diminishes, the detail must be simplified. Figure 8, showing the well-known Henry II. chimney piece from the "Chateau de Villeroy," is an excellent example of several of the above cases.

The law just expressed, *i.e.*, that as scale diminishes, detail must be simplified, is exceedingly important, for only by its observance are the exceptions spoken of farther back made possible.

There are many objects that cannot be portrayed at their real, or yet at their natural, relative sizes, such as the sun, moon and stars, prows of vessels, masts, military emblems, cannon, and in a heraldic device, towers and other similar picturings. All of these elements may be used, nevertheless, provided the detail is simplified. It is well to conventionalize such subjects; indeed, only thus can the sun, stars, etc., be indicated.

Again we see in some of the classic groups of sculpture (the Laocoon and the group of Niobe are examples cited by Mayeux with regard to this) the principal figure made larger in proportion to the others than nature would warrant; nowadays, although this is done less commonly, in certain cases it is still useful. (The tympanum of a classic pediment, with the central

FIG. 8. — HENRY II. CHIMNEY PIECE OF THE CHATEAU DE VILLEROY.
(Now at the Museé du Louvre.)

figure usually of heroic size as compared to the others; or a monumental statue, a smaller figure being introduced for the interpretation of an idea, or even merely to give scale.)

In all such cases the same law holds good. Here the enlarged figures must have more detail given them; the hem of a robe, treated with brocaded designs, perhaps, or the shield of a warrior, embossed with bas-reliefs. And with regard to this it may be well to remark that "detail" does not mean a fine, or finically indicated portrayal, for the elements may, and if the monument is a large one to be viewed from a distance, should be treated in the most simple manner. It becomes plain why mechanical reductions and enlargements are so bad. In such reductions the same amount of detail is crowded into a smaller space.

If two Greek frets, of different dimensions, are used in the same composition, the smaller must be the simpler. If two entablatures are used in a building, the smaller might well be composed of two members — architrave and cornice, say — instead of three, as would be the main entablature.

In a large composition, if a certain form, a pediment perhaps, has been used in the principal motive, we should carefully avoid repeating it, at a smaller scale, as a submotive. This extends to the most insignificant elements. If dentils are indicated in a main cornice, they should be omitted from a smaller one. Always avoid introducing a motive or element which may be the baby of another. The only exception to this is for graduated decorations (see page 116).

We may also, inversely, deduce from this the method of retaining the same decorative scale in different portions of the same suite. Suppose several panels, of individual lengths (Fig. 9) are to form a frieze. In the first of these panels we introduce certain elements

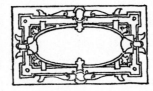

Fig. 9.

making a complete design; in the second we must not attempt to enlarge these elements to fill the greater space, but must use them at their original size, adding new elements of like character to complete the panel. In the smaller panels some of the elements are merely left out.

This principle, which should extend throughout commercial art, is, unhappily, but too often ignored. Books of a set, furniture for the same room; in fact, any group of decorative objects should have common elements of common dimensions.

4. *The Requirement of the Visual Distance as governed by the Ensemble*

The detail, as well as the general scheme of a composition, should be legible at the distance from which the beholder is expected to view it.

This distance is governed by the visual angle and by

F

the total size of the composition.   Thus, in figure 10, if $EBC = ECB$, d and d' are defined by the sizes of BEC and BC.   The scale of a large composition would,

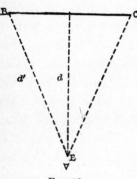

FIG. 10.

therefore, be entirely different from that of a small one (BEC is really fixed in size, within certain limits) ; that of a building would be quite unlike that of an illuminated manuscript.

As an instance of the kind of fault easily committed : the bronze gentleman on the top of the tower of one of our well-known public buildings holds a carefully engraved scroll, legible to nobody, and only to be guessed at by visitors to the roof.   Milan, Cologne, the Certosa of Pavia, and other such buildings are older examples of like mistakes of scale, the detail being too fine to be grasped from the distance at which the ensemble should be seen.

Nice distinctions of scale may be made by an observant artist.   In a public hall, the rug to be looked at from the end of the room or from a gallery would have a much simpler and broader design than would that of a lady's boudoir.   The decoration of a theater would be larger in scale than that of a private house. Also, the scale of the decorations at the top of a tall building would, as already suggested in discussion of wasted ornament (see page 34), be of a different scale from those at the bottom.   Apparently, the best manner of composing a twenty-story office building is to place one or two stories in the entablature, and so on. Thus the first and last of the requirements for good scale are satisfied; the human unit, as evinced by the windows, is retained, while the decorative motive is made broad enough to "carry" from a great height.

It may be well to note in connection with this that architecture, sculpture, indeed any bit of decoration appears smaller than it actually is, when placed out of doors. Because of this, and to make sure that the composition will "carry," it is well to keep the detail of exterior work large in scale. The usual height of the so-called life-size statue is seven or eight feet, according to its placing near or farther from the eye.

As a general résumé of this most important question, "scale," the elements of a composition relating to human needs or to material requirements, must be exactly of the size suited to these requirements; the portrayal of natural objects must not be in discord with nature, while the general decorative scheme of the design, together with the detail employed, must be in harmony with the total size and character of the whole composition.

To give scale to a composition, providing there are no faults to eliminate:

1. Human elements may be introduced.

2. Constructive elements may be made more evident.

3. A decorative portrayal of natural objects, whose scale is apparent, may be introduced.

4. Submotives may be added to the principal motives, to give a comparison.

5. The general size of the detail may be reduced everywhere.

CHAPTER II

BEFORE leaving the general for the special in taking up different applications of the foregoing laws of composition, a word may be said about the manner of analyzing a composition.

Artists usually approach the arrangement of a subject by one of two paths. A first class of men work synthetically, showing a natural tendency to reason about the arrangements which will best suit the requirements of a program; another class work from sentiment, drawing in something, which, if it does not finally strike the right chord, is either altered or erased.

As suggested in remarks at the end of Part I., the method pursued by the men who reason is a sound one. It is more direct and sure. Unluckily, some personal verve of imagination may be lost by a too exclusive adherence thereto, for though an artist is an intellectual as well as a sensitive being, he is not a mathematical machine. A combination of both methods, therefore, is good.

In other words (allowance being made for individuality of temperament), after the general scheme has been reasoned out and all logical needs observed, we may permit ourselves free rein to fill the composition with original bits, remembering simply that a thing's being *different* does not make it *personal*. After having put ourselves into the work to the fullest extent, we must, however, return to the first method, analyze what lies before us and show our strength of character by cutting out everything which violates the sound laws in which we believe.

At the beginning of the second part of "The Fine Arts," G. Baldwin Brown suggests that we see in nature tones, textures, colors, forms, and lines. In viewing a particular object from one spot, these impressions are created by certain defined portions of space, which must in consequence have a shape. These shapes either will (like the oblong) or will not (like the square) follow some general line or direction. Moreover, if they lead from one to another, as the laws of composition say they sometimes should, a direction will thereby be expressed.

We may, then, study the general massing of a composition, and the general massing is what makes an arrangement fundamentally good or bad, without regard to the particular manner — tone, texture, color, interior form of the individual element, or simple outline — in which its elements impress us, merely examining or indicating the relative positions and shapes of these elements, and noting especially the contrast or continuity of the directions to which they conform.

To analyze the general masses of a pictorial composition the easiest trick is to put the eyes out of focus. A little practice in looking past the object one wishes to blur, and at a distant object, will soon make the action almost unconscious. Persons who are farsighted need only take off their glasses and relax the muscles of the eye; those who are nearsighted have but to stand away from the drawing. Unless one is accustomed to looking through a microscope or telescope, it is better to cover one eye; otherwise one sees double.

The blurred shapes arising from this experiment are the fundamental elements which must compose. We shall pass in review the different general classes in which they may be grouped. As the comparative directions of these motives are the important factors in their composition, the directing lines are usually all that will be considered.

Usual Arrangements of Pictorial Compositions

The laws of composition tell us [1] that the more we reduce the number of secondary focal points in a design, the greater will be the effect produced. Therefore, the strongest, as well as the simplest, composition will be that which has but one focal point — the climax and its accompaniments.

First, then, we shall examine the unsymmetrical composition having but one focal point.

The application of our general laws is here so simple that we need only make a few suggestions. Broadly speaking, there are three methods (we may derive them from what was said of the composition of lines on page 45) by which the accompanying elements are made to relate to their focal point; they may lead into it, form a frame around it or radiate from it. The second two of these methods usually imply a symmetrical ar-

---

[1] This does not follow what Mr. Ruskin suggests in his "Elements of Drawing and Composition."

rangement; so we shall discuss them with the next class of compositions. The first of the three methods is the one most used in unsymmetrical, informal work; therefore, broadly speaking, in designs of the first group the main lines of the subelements must lead into the climax.

With regard to the fourth law of composition, in such an example as Whistler's portrait of his mother, or the Holbein Head of Erasmus, more space should be left in front of the face than behind. The features give especial interest to one side. In the light of the fifth law, we readily see how disastrous would be lines near a frame, that might establish a motive parallel to it; parallel motives without a liaison do not compose. This preoccupation in regard to a design's composing with its border should exist in all cases where a frame is to be used.

Beside portraits in profile, etc., decorative panels with one figure not on axis, the greater number of smaller unsymmetrical paintings, certain monuments and most examples of modern sculpture come within this group.

Second, the symmetrical composition with but one focal point and one axis.

To reduce the number of subelements, an axis of symmetry (being really a succession of minor focal points, or a focal point extended in one direction) should coincide with a major focal point. The three methods of composing the lines of elements, spoken of in the discussion of the preceding class, in this class are equally useful.

For an illustration of them see *A*, *B*, and *C*, Fig. 11. In all of these arrangements the climax, that it may answer to *b* of the first law (page 42), must not be too near either the top or the bottom of the composition. If the design has a "head" and "base" — such designs usually do — the lines near the base would best form either a horizontal succession, or else themselves be horizontal or horizontally inclined. This is

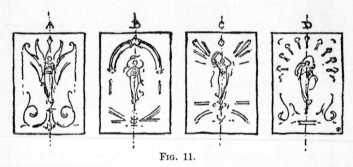

the one exception where a motive of a composition may be made parallel to the frame. Even then it should be broken or limited. Raffaelle's "Sistine Madonna" is an excellent example of a design composed under the second method of this class (Fig. 12). It may be analyzed as the diagram shows.

There are many compositions formed in part under one of the three methods of Fig. 11, and in part under another. At times, a single element may come under the head of two of them at once, as in Fig. 11, *D*, where the semicircular suite is formed of motives that radiate, and yet, in their ensemble, form a frame. The general scheme of decoration at the end of a barrel-vaulted room is often treated thus.

If the design, belonging to this or any class, is to fit into a circular or elliptical frame, the lines near the edge of the composition, unless radiating directly from the center, should not be straight (exception may sometimes be made for a short base line, especially if softened or broken by details); they would best lead out of the frame into the central portion of the

FIG. 12.

design, as in Botticelli's "Madonna Incoronata." A decided horizontal base line is to be avoided here. If there are no definite lines near the edge of such a curved frame, the interior design may have its outer edge either blended into the background or made of curves or lines in different directions, that there may be no unpleasant feeling of parallelism with the frame. The composition for a medal might come within this group, as do circular full-face portraits.

Third, we take up the unsymmetrical composition with an axis of symmetry passing through the climax.

Here it is well to balance the long accompanying motive which necessarily occurs on one side of the axis by a more condensed one on the other. Lateral elevations of buildings often come under this head, being composed of a symmetrical pavilion with an accompanying long wing behind. An entrance or important decorative motive on the main façade of the building will establish the equilibrium (Fig. 13).

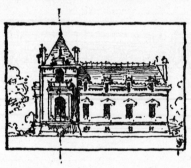

FIG. 13.

In connection with this it may be remarked that an architect should remember his building is to be seen in perspective, and if he makes his principal elevation a symmetrical one, he should make the lateral elevation unsymmetrical.

Mr. John Beverly Robinson says, in an article on composition:[1] "It is one of the indications of the superiority of the artistic sense of the Greeks, to our own, that their effortless perception of odd and even extended to so many more things than does ours. A

[1] See *The Architectural Record*, 1898–99, p. 112.

Greek took as much care to put fourteen, or sixteen, or eighteen intercolumniations on the side of a building, in order to avoid a central opening, as we take to put the door in the middle of a room."

Fourth, we shall examine the composition with one focal point and with two axes of symmetry at right angles to each other, both passing through the middle of the composition.

Naturally, the focal point will here be at the intersection of the axes, and will itself be symmetrical in

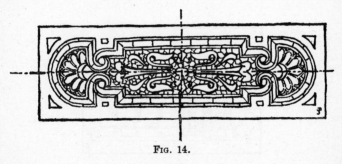

Fig. 14.

regard to each. There should be no top or bottom to such a design. Certain rugs, some ceiling decorations, rose windows, etc., come under this head. There may be a case of this group where the accompanying elements have special ties to unite them with the main motive. These ties must be symmetrically placed with regard to both axes (Fig. 14).

Fifth in order comes the symmetrical composition, having a second axis which does not pass through the middle of the composition.

Again, the climax will be at the intersection of the axes, the latter at right angles to each other. The principal axis, defining the composition as symmetrical, draws its name from that, and should always be the more important. It need not be the more extended. It may be either vertical or horizontal. In both cases the composition will have a direction. The climax may be above, below, to right or left of the middle of the composition; but not too near the edge, nor

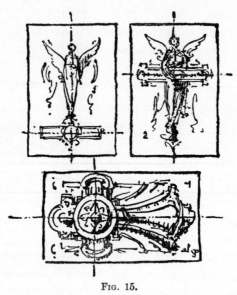

FIG. 15.

just off the middle. About one third from one end (two thirds from the other) will be a good position. Such a composition might be adopted for a vertical panel or for the decoration of a book cover or album. In each case a direction is implied (Fig. 15).

Sixth, there might be a rather unusual case of an unsymmetrical composition with two axes, either equal or unequal, either cutting the climax or merely radiating from it on one side, either at right angles to each other or not.

In any event, the climax would be at the meeting of the axes ; and if these do not make an angle of 90° there should be a special reason for it (such as an attempt to make the design fit better in a frame). Moreover, the angle of the axes should not be too acute, nor yet just off the right angle (Fig. 16, *a*). When the axes are equal, a symmetrical figure really results, with an implied third and main axis bisecting the angle which they make (Fig. 16, *c*). *b*, Fig. 16, is so forced as not to be very good. It would be better treated as an unsymmetrical composition without any axes (the symmetry of the present axes destroyed), or with only one, as are many lateral elevations (see Fig. 13).

Seventh, the symmetrical composition having a main axis and two minor axes parallel to it, the secondary motives being adjacent to the principal motive.

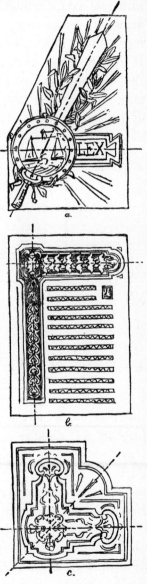

Fig. 16.

This makes a three-motive composition. As we know, parallel motives do not compose unless some of their elements, or foreign elements, serve as a tie. The most successful method for tying together the secondary and principal motives of this seventh class is to make common some of the elements of the motives.

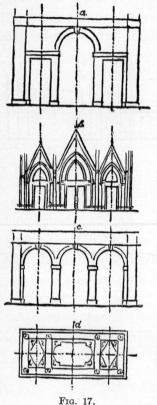

FIG. 17.

The sketches of Fig. 17 will show this treatment.

Eighth, the same composition with a main axis of symmetry at right angles to the first.

The manner of uniting the motives would be the same. If a foreign tie, or ties exist, it or they should be symmetrically placed with regard to the main axes (Fig. 17, *d*).

Ninth, the symmetrical composition having a main axes and two minor secondary axis parallel to it, the secondary motives being separated from the principal motive.

Such an arrangement should be used when a composition is so large, or exists in such different planes, that its separate motives are to be seen independently, as well as in the ensemble. Thus the three motives *A, B,* and *B′* of *a,* Fig. 18, will, in perspective, come within the ninth class, the submotives being separated from the climax by the wings C, C'.

That the minor motives may unite with the climax in a five-element composition of this class, especially if all five elements are in the same plane (Fig. 18, *b*), the intervening elements should contrast with the

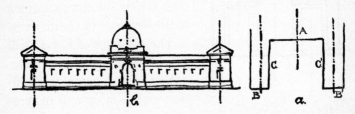

FIG. 18.

main motives in direction, arrangement, and size; they should tie in with the main motives; they should create as little as possible axes of their own. Be it repeated, the secondary motives should never look like babies of the climax (see "scale," page 66).

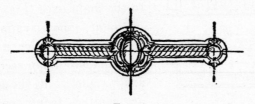

FIG. 19.

Tenth, we have a repetition of the preceding case with the addition of a main axis of symmetry at right angles to the others.

Fig. 19 shows this, the manner of composing it being the same as that of class nine with the additional need

of placing any ties symmetrically in regard to the new
main axis.

Eleventh, we have the same case as in the ninth class,
with unsymmetrical motives on each end, a composition of seven elements (Fig. 20). This should only be
used in long elevations, etc.

Twelfth, the symmetrical composition with several
subaxes, parallel and perpendicular to the main axis.

Large plans are nearly always of this class. Fig.
73, M. Henri Deglane's successful design in the competition for the Grand Prix de Rome of the French "In-

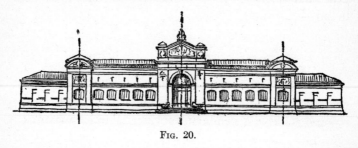

FIG. 20.

stitut," 1881, is a well-known example. In attacking
such a problem, the more the number of axes is reduced,
the better it will be.

Thirteenth, the unsymmetrical composition with two
principal focal points.

Such an arrangement would only be used where a
dominant idea (the program) makes it imperative.
Titian's "Sacred and Profane Love" is an example
of this. The result must, of course, be less concentrated than that given by a composition with only one
focal point; although in such a work as Titian's the
contrast of the figures accentuates each. Even here,

we are forced to glance from one figure to the other, —
to divide the attention between them.

In making a design of this kind the artist must remember that each climax while remaining adequately
separated, should evidently relate to the other, and that
the lines of the subelements should lead up to and
connect them. Otherwise two compositions, instead
of one, will result.

A corridor or long building connecting two different
but equally important pavilions, in elevation, would
give such a composition (Fig. 21). This often occurs
in side elevations.

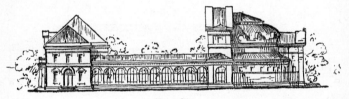

FIG. 21.

Fourteenth, the symmetrical composition with two
equal principal motives not widely separated.

Like the last considered class, this offers a solution
which is not concentrated, and therefore should also
only be used for the sake of the program.

It may be good where a crowd or stream of people
is to enter a building by one door and come out by
another — the railroad station (Fig. 22, *a*), for example.
It is well to place a decorative motive on the pier between such bays. This concentrates the attention. It
might be said that this also takes the composition out
of the present class, by establishing a main axis.

G

Fifteenth. We have still one more case of the symmetrical composition showing two equal climaxes, separated by a long motive (Fig. 22, *b*).

It would now be a mistake to try to concentrate the attention on a spot between the climaxes, in that they could never form one group, and the addition of a

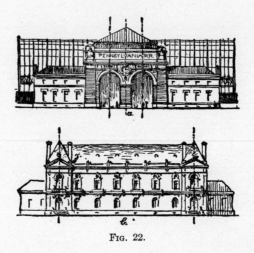

Fig. 22.

fictitious point of interest would merely multiply the number of focal points.

We cannot pretend in fifteen groups, or classes of compositions, to have exhausted the subject, but having noted the most important combinations, we may hope to have given suggestions which will serve for others of like character. And these suggestions are, after all, only the outcome of the main laws of composition. By a strict adherence to the latter, even such a difficult problem as the one presented in M. Pascal's famous Grand Prix plan (Fig. 23) can be successfully solved.

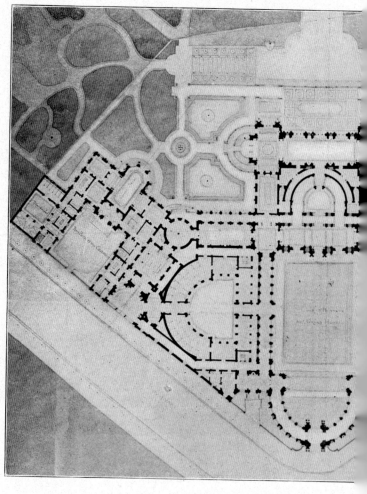

Fig. 23. — Grand Prix Plan of M. Pascal

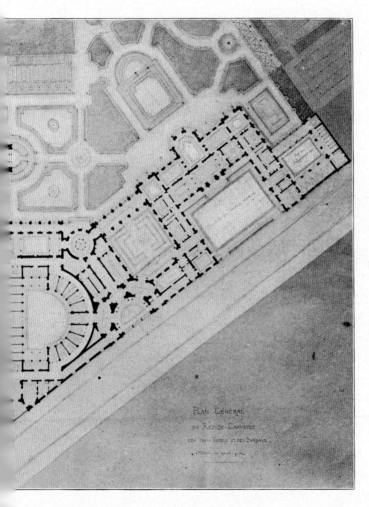

PLAN GÉNÉRAL
DU REZ-DE-CHAVSÉE
DES TROIS HOTELS ET DES BVREAVX

IS HOTELS POUR TROIS FRÉRES BANQUIERS."

PART III

CHAPTER I

DECORATIVE APPLICATION OF THE LAWS OF COMPOSITION

IN "La Composition Décorative,"[1] M. Henri Mayeux has treated the practical arrangement of decoration in such a complete and masterly manner that I shall refer to him those readers who want more detail than present space allows.

Following somewhat the plan adopted in "La Composition Décorative," we shall take up first the study of the *form* of decorative motives, then the study of *decoration*, irrespective of the form on which it is placed, and lastly, the application of decoration to form.

1. *Form*

Considering their form, we may divide decorative motives into two groups: (*a*) those which have two dimensions, height and width, and (*b*) those which have three dimensions, height, width and thickness.

(*a*) The requirements of motives belonging to the first of these two groups lie in the shape of the silhouette. Recurring to the laws already laid down,

[1] Paris, Librairies Imprimeries Réunies, Ancienne Maison Quantin.

we remember that what is undecided is never agreeable (see Part I., page 25). So all silhouettes should have marked characteristics. A succession of mouldings ought not to form a wavering and unmeaning line; there should be no question about the general form of any contour.

A square ought to appear exactly square, while rectangles which are not square must never be almost so. The same is true of circles and ovals, while a diamond should be elongated enough not to look like a square on one corner. The most agreeable proportion for a rectangle is supposed to be given by making the longer side equal to the diagonal of the square erected on the shorter.

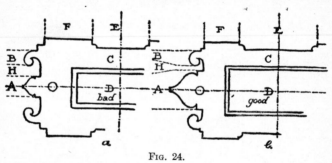

Fig. 24.

Again, the laws just referred to show us that unlike succeeding motives of equal dimensions are bad; and when we remember that one of the elements of a composition is to dominate the others we realize why *a* of Fig. 24 is displeasing. *A* is too nearly equal to *B*, as is *C* to *D*, and *A*, the principal motive, does not dominate. Also, projecting motives should not be equal to the retreating elements which separate them, as are *F* and *E* or *B* and *H*.

The fact that indecision is distressing will guide us in the general arrangement of our silhouette. If we have chosen a symmetrical scheme, each element

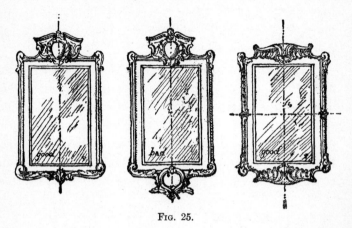

Fig. 25.

will repeat itself; but where an axis of symmetry does not exist, neither the details, nor the general mass (the latter is often the more difficult to keep in mind)

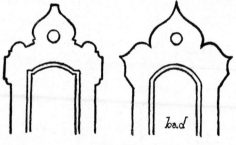

Fig. 26.

will be similar. Fig. 25 shows this in relation to a horizontal axis.

We should avoid silhouettes which are too broken

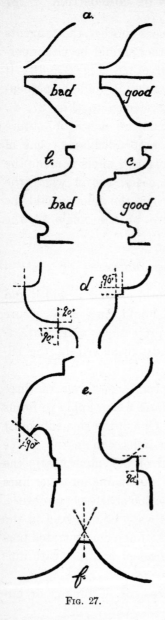

FIG. 27.

(as in some of the Flemish work) with an equal amount of decoration everywhere. Unbroken lines should be introduced to give contrast. For the same reason a silhouette must not be composed entirely of straight lines, else it becomes rigid, brutal and uninteresting.

Last of all, do not make silhouettes with angles, either protruding or reëntrant, which are too acute or obtuse. That lines may contrast and compose, we remember that the angles they make should be as near 90° as possible. Also, acute and sharp angles are, in many cases, both difficult to construct and to protect from injury; they give one a feeling of being pointed, painful to touch, and, on the whole, unpleasant (see Fig. 26).

Curves which are flat or approach the straight line are bad (Fig. 27, a). Usually composite curved lines formed (without breaks) of more than two elements are bad (Fig.

27, *b*).   When one curve succeeds another, the tangents
at the ends which come together should be either perpendicular or parallel to each other (Fig. 27, *d*).   If
there is a fillet between such curves, it would be perpendicular to the tangents just referred to (Fig. 27, *d*).
If, however, the tangents make an acute or obtuse
angle, the break should be perpendicular to one of
them (Fig. 27, *e*) : the more exposed angle is made the
less acute — and this in all cases, except where the
curves repeat each other, when the fillet would be
perpendicular to the bisectrice of the angle of the
tangents (Fig. 27, *f*).

(*b*) Forms of Three Dimensions

In a composition where depth, as well as width and
height, is a factor, the artist should, first of all, insure
that the design which his projections accentuate is
in harmony with that already displayed in the silhouette.

The laws governing the profiles of forms of three
dimensions are the same as those which apply to forms
having but two dimensions.   One of the elements must
dominate ; there must be no indecision in the choice
of the "partie" (symmetrical or unsymmetrical) ; the
lines and shapes must not be mistakable for other lines
or shapes ; angles must not be too sharp or too obtuse,
and a good balancing must always be observed in the
joint use of curved and straight lines, concentrated portions of decoration being placed in contrast with uniform or undecorated portions.

In the comparison of spaces, or of broken or unbroken surfaces, in like or unlike projections, the laws of composition may be applied in the same manner.

If two similar motives exist, one over the other — this occurs in some bookshelves, or in a buffet — they should be exact repetitions one of the other (Fig. 28).

In regard to mouldings: flat cymas, etc., are sometimes used, as they seem to express more strength than a greatly distorted surface; but even here the recommendation holds good not to make a curved surface which may resemble a plane. In a suite of

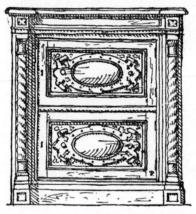

FIG. 28.

mouldings it is well to recall the projections of important members of different groups. The custom of making the stilobate of the base of a column come exactly over the shaft of the pedestal is an example of this. (See in Fig. 29 an example of a good suite of mouldings.)

In designing mouldings which cut under and do not show in elevation, care must be taken that the realiza-

tion of the design does not contain unpleasant surprises.   In Fig. 30, at A and
B, the tangents a' and b' should be either
parallel or normal to the succeeding important elements, c' and d', or possibly
to e and f.   If the angles A and B are
too acute, they should be altered, as in
the second figure at A' and B'.

Of course, one suite of mouldings
would never be blindly run into another
suite at right angles to it.   When unlike sets of mouldings form an angle, the
best method is to place a plain block at
the intersection, either arranged so that
each set will end against it, or so conceived that it will coincide with a group
of members of the higher set and receive
all of those of the lower.   Sometimes a
very simple element — usually it must

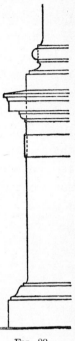

Fig. 29.

be a vertical or only slightly inclined plain member of

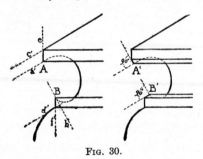

Fig. 30.

one of the suites — may be large enough to receive the
more complex members of the other suite; in which

case the supplementary block becomes unnecessary. There is seldom a disadvantage in introducing the plain stone; for it acts as an agreeable foil to the more contorted forms of the mouldings.

A quality, necessary to all objects in full relief, is stability, and this need must be met in appearance, as well as in reality. For instance, a clock, a prize cup or even a student lamp may have concentrated portions of metal on one side which actually balance the larger, hollow portions on the other; but if they seem unequal, if one fears that the object may topple over, the design is faulty. Even flat compositions, decorations, etc., should, whenever verticality is suggested, seem to be supported or suspended from a point in the same vertical with the center of gravity of the shape. The unsymmetrical Louis XV. cartouche, shown in Fig. 31, should be balanced sufficiently on the side opposite the figure to maintain its apparent equilibrium. In other words, whenever a design appears subject to the laws of gravity, absolute obedience to these laws must be evident.

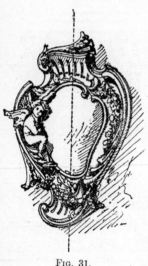

Fig. 31.

A special case having something in common with this may occur in the treatment of objects of three dimensions, where a vertical axis exists, with a triangular or pentangular, etc., plan. Here, because the object is only symmetrical when seen from certain directions, it is unwise to place above it another form which is symmetrical in all directions. Fig. 32 shows how disastrous may be the result of crowning a triangular monument with a dome. Indeed, it is well to treat the monument having a triangular plan as though it were unsymmetrical, placing a decorative element in the middle of each face, to balance the projection of the opposite corner. Thus is the appearance of stability maintained.

2. *Decoration*

Examining different kinds of decoration, with the sources from which they may be derived, we find two great classes comprising :

A. Motives which represent an object.

B. Motives which are merely a combination of lines or forms.

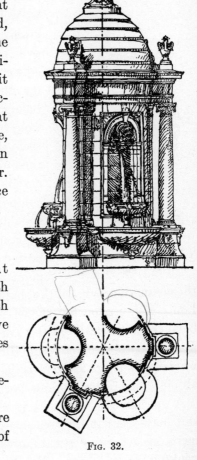

FIG. 32.

A. Motives which represent an object may again

be divided; this time (according to the method of
their representation) into four general classes;[1] *i.e.*,
(*a*) the objects may be depicted in a natural manner

FIG. 33.

and arranged informally; (*b*) they may be depicted
in a natural manner, but arranged in a formal com-

---

[1] Mayeux suggests only three general classes into which motives
may be divided, considering *c* and *d* under the same head.

FIG. 33.

position; (*c*) they may be depicted in a conventional manner and arranged informally; (*d*) they may be conventionalized and arranged in a formal composition. Also, a mixed method may exist where a representation of one kind is introduced as a detail in a representation of another kind (Fig. 33, *e*).

(*a* and *b*) Here we need few suggestions, as the general laws of composition show us where to concentrate the interest and how to balance and keep our arrangement in scale, etc. (Fig. 33). We have only to choose and carefully depict the best of what nature has to offer. The Renaissance offers many fine examples of this kind of decoration.

(*c* and *d*) It is in the third and fourth divisions where the elements are conventionalized that we find the most truly decorative expression of art. And this, I think, is easily understood. Decoration, pure and simple, exists primarily to please the eye by beautifying a particular object or place. It must usually have little or no individuality of its own, because it is the accessory of another individuality. It must always be subservient to the object or place it decorates. Therefore it is that records of nature are somewhat out of place when used for decorative purposes. They are too personal and assert themselves. It is true that we enjoy, in a decorative sense, conventionalized elements of nature where the characteristics are truthfully retained, — the more truthfully, the better, — but when these elements become portraits, instead of suggestions, they should be by themselves in a frame or on a pedestal. Moreover, except in the case of wax flowers and similar imitations, where the only art shown is that in the fashioning (the art of a machine rather than of a man), all representations of nature or portraits must be, to some extent, conventional. Who can give the actual effect of sunlight by putting paint on a piece of canvas? Therefore, where it is not the aim of the artist to catch and mark the particular phase or effect of a model, he would better keep himself as far as possible from the realistic; he will thus gain in "frankness" as well as in the decorative feeling.

It may be asked as an objection to this, "Why is it that those designs which suggest the characteristics of nature are yet useful for decorations, are even more pleasing, perhaps, than purely geometrical forms?"

At the beginning of this discussion of composition we said that that work of art is the broadest which brings into play all the faculties of the observer. It is probably for this reason that forms which remind us of previously experienced pleasures are, in that, more to our taste than those which suggest nothing. We must remember that in all branches of art there is some one characteristic which must dominate the others. In our present study it is, as we began by saying, the characteristic which gives beauty to a particular part of a particular composition.

A maxim for decorators is that in their work all suggestion of relief or depression, not actually existent in the surface of the finished design, should be eschewed. Hence perspective lines and distance effects ought, in mural paintings, etc., only to be introduced with the greatest care. A conventionalization of such effects is all that can be tolerated. In other decorative work, excepting perhaps mural tapestries, and possibly stained glass, it is better never to use any perspective. It is easy to realize the truth of this, for whatever the subject depicted in a mural painting, it is evident the wall should still show that it is a solid plane substance, quite able to support the ceiling or vault. Also, we may be certain a carpet would not reassure the visitor were he deluded into thinking he must walk upon spear points, or perhaps fall through a hole into infinite space, while few men would care to tread upon the delicate form of a beautiful child, no matter how unusual or original might seem its presence upon the floor.

All objects, not in themselves too conventional, may be conventionalized.

This is done by accentuating the characteristics of the object or of the species to which the object belongs, leaving out all unnecessary details. Mayeux says, in speaking of the conventionalization of plants: [1] "C'est d'ailleurs l'allure même des végétaux qui indiquera le sens ou l'artiste doit s'engager; ainsi on accentuera la symétrie et même la rigidité, si la plante l'exprime déjà, ou au contraire la souplesse et la flexibilité si la nature présente cette tendance. . . . En un mot, il s'agit d'affirmer le mouvement déjà ébauché par la nature même et de remplacer l'attrait de la vérité dans le dessin et la couleur par le caractère de la silhouette et la simplicité de la facture."

[1] "La Composition Décorative," p. 50.

We must be careful, when following this advice, to avoid accentuating the freaks of a particular model. These can never be characteristic of the plant itself.

Persian art gives us an almost limitless list of examples of conventionalization; in studying its masterpieces we realize that simple flowers are the best to choose as models for our work. Other sources for inspiration are Egypt, Greece and Japan.

In conventionalizing animals it is safer to be more or less extreme, possibly merely filling in the silhouette with a flat, characteristic, but not too naturalistic tone, and omitting all modeling. The Japanese, however, be the result intentional or unintentional, have proved that an animal may be conventionalized and yet be most delicately and beautifully detailed.

In portraying the sun, moon and stars, water, fire, etc., it is hardly possible to do more than present a symbolical rendering. Thus the sun of Louis XIV. is a face with rays emanating in all directions, while the rays of light, so much used in ecclesiastical architecture of the Louis XV. period — in St. Roch at Paris and other similar churches — are only barely suggestive of the sun's breaking out from behind a cloud. The three crescents, interlaced, of Dianne de Poictiers, is another well-known example of symbolical representation; indeed, heraldic devices in general are rich mines of suggestion.

The objects which are the result of man's inventive genius, properly represented, may come in aid of the designer. Implements of war, of the arts and sciences, and architecture itself, all lend themselves as elements

H

of decoration. The methods of conventionalization are identical with those used for natural objects; the leaving out of unnecessary details, the use of a simple suggestive silhouette, etc. In this province, the laws relative to scale must be kept continually in mind.

When treating architecture, it is often well to reduce or lighten its elements, even making the whole purely fantastic. Of course, the same feeling must exist throughout the example, for if a colonnette of reduced proportion support a vase or emblem of the ordinary size, or if a volute of sturdy growth serve as base for a delicate spindle and fairy-like entablature, the result will hardly be agreeable. The student should examine some of the Pompeian fresco decorations, where the rendering of architecture plays so prominent and attractive a part. In this direction Renaissance work is less good, although some of the early Renaissance stained glass shows a very beautiful treatment of architecture.

As a warning against too great extremes: it is never well to push the conventionalization of an object so far as to lose the primitive characteristic charm of the subject; otherwise, to use the words of M. Mayeux,[1] "la modification *trop forcé* ou l'exécution *trop sommaire* finit par lasser, et l'intérêt s'évanouit." The artist should familiarize himself with nature, and in his study draw its manifold manifestations as exactly as possible. Thus will he retain, in his final interpretations, the innate sentiment of his model.

B. Motives which are merely a combination of lines

---

[1] "La Composition Décorative," p. 65.

or forms may sometimes vaguely suggest real objects ; but, nevertheless, they have a right to be considered by themselves.

Thus the running ornament composed of a single line, reminds one of a string or fine cord tying itself into knots and then finding its way out again ; or perchance it simulates a growing vine, stretching out its tendrils and clinging to sturdier points, while a coiling or wavering flat band seems to represent a thong of leather or a ribbon. Usually this suggestive quality of pure line or form is agreeable from the decorative point of view.

Geometrical figures and designs often owe their origin to a perception of the above on the part of the designer. But the free volutes and spirals of the Rococo (Louis XV.) styles are derived, in great measure without such aid, from the artist's imagination.

Arabian art and Moorish art offer the best sources to which the student may go for models of impersonal decoration. The Moors, not being permitted by their religious prejudices to depict flowers, animals, or figures, necessarily had recourse to combinations of line and mass only ; and their cousins of the East, although more free, seem not to be behind them in beauty of similar design.

Before going on to the study of the application of decoration to form, we may consider two elements which appear in nearly every decoration, viz. :

The relation or continuity which exists between the different motives of the decoration.

The relation of the decoration to its background.

CONTINUITY OF MOTIVES

We have lately remarked that almost all ornaments, if not directly, at least indirectly, remind us of some object : that which is represented by a line (iron work, engraved work, etc.) of a cord, or vine ; that which is flat, but has width as well as length (the classic interlaced ornament and Greek fret, also French Renaissance cartouches and scroll work, etc., down to the Henry IV. period) of leather work, or of a ribbon ; that which has relief, and is modeled, of an infinity of objects.

M. Mayeux suggests this as the reason for the need of certain ties between different motives in a suite. For instance, in iron work a bolt or rivet is needed to hold together two pieces which touch ; so in an ornament which reminds us of iron work, even unintentionally, we feel, through analogy, the need of a suggested rivet.

That there is much truth of sentiment in this theory is evident ; but true or not, if we turn to the general laws which govern composition, we see another reason for the existence of ties, in the craving the eye has for proper contrast of line.

I think that, in general, we would better hold to the broad laws, as when motives cross each other no tie is needed ; and to carry out the simile of the vine we should have to imitate objectionable lines and connections, induced in a plant by laws of gravity, with which we, in our compositions, would possibly have nothing to do.

We may study the relation of motives under three different heads :

(*a*) The motives do not touch;

(*b*) they are tangent;

(*c*) they cross.

(*a*) If the motives do not touch, an intermediate motive should, usually, be introduced.

If the original motives accentuate a certain direction,

FIG. 34.

the intermediate motive should accentuate another in contrast with it (Fig. 34, *a*). At the point of contact the intermediate motive should be either normal or tangent to the original motive (Fig. 34, *b* and *c*).

FIG. 35.

(*b*) If the motives touch, a tie should be introduced. This usually takes the form of a short normal to the motives, being placed at their point of contact (Fig. 35, *a* and *b*). Sometimes, however, it circles around the point of contact or is otherwise disposed; in that case the lines of the tie and the original motive may be either tangent or normal to each other (Fig. 35, *c*). Sometimes the tie not only simulates, but actually is

a fastening which holds the elements together. Its
counterpart in architecture is the impost moulding
at the springing of an arch. We remember that the
eye always feels the need of a normal of some sort when

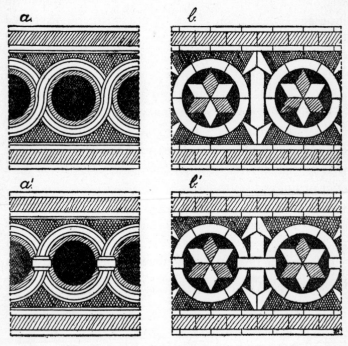

Fig. 36.

parallelism occurs between the lines of two motives, or
when — as with a curve and straight line — one element is continued by another.

There are two exceptions to the foregoing rule; in
them the tie may be omitted. They occur when motives cover each other, forming an interlaced decoration; and when, as in mosaic, the motives seem fitted

one into the other, built into a space as are blocks in a box. Even here, a break or normal, introduced as a contrast at the point of contact of the motives, is a welcome addition (Fig. 36, *a, a', b, b'*). When an interlaced decoration is used, care must be exercised that the elements alternate, one first in front of, and then behind, the other, as in an actual plaited design.

It is often unwise to allow a motive surrounded by a frame to become tangent to the frame; in such a case the design has a tendency to appear crowded. Mayeux suggests, as a preferable solution, that where the size of the frame is given and the motive cannot well be reduced, it be augmented and allowed to pass over or under the frame.

(*c*) If the motives cross, no tie is necessary; but in order that a good contrast of line exist, the directions taken by the elements at the point of intersection should be as nearly perpendicular to each other as possible (Fig. 37).

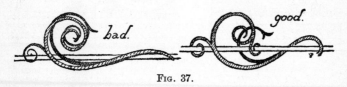

FIG. 37.

Here again, when a plaiting or interlacing occurs, the motives should alternate as in nature. This applies not only to lines and curves, etc., but to the combining of any decorative design, whatever its composition — invented objects, plants or even figures.

If the elements of the design definitely suggest natural objects, they should, in arrangement, follow the

plan to which their prototypes would adhere. Even
in a suite of spirals and volutes, portraying a vine
indefinitely, and without intention on the part of the

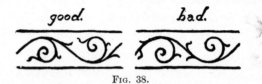

FIG. 38.

artist, it is best to make the growth of the design in
one direction (Fig. 38). We have already noted the
necessity of observing the requirements of the law of

FIG. 39.

gravity, whenever a composition suggests verticality.
If objects are pictured standing upon a base or hanging
from a definite point, they must be shown in the posi-

tion which the originals would need occupy. If a garland is portrayed, it should have the curve of a real garland; if figures are introduced, with but faint semblance of reality given by the modeling, still the equilibrium of each should be carefully maintained. Fig. 39 shows the absurdity of violating this apparently evident truth. We may only turn from the usual aspect of nature when marked conventionalization or some other explanation (such, perhaps, as the implication of supernatural power in flying or floating subjects) sets the mind at rest. Moreover, all figures which appear to stand on something should have a visible and adequate support. Any violation of these laws — indeed, of any natural law — is a negation of art.

BACKGROUNDS

We may, once more, follow the lead of "La Composition Décorative,"[1] and divide our subject into two parts, examining first the relation of intensity, or value, between the subject and its ground, and second, their relation as regards surface.

As a starting point for the study of the first of these divisions, Mayeux cites a well-known fact, i.e., "That a white detail with a black ground will look larger than a similar black detail on a white ground."[2] Therefore it is important to decide a priori whether the subject of a design is to be relieved in dark or light. The advantage of adopting the scheme of the light

[1] Pages 155 to 165.
[2] See also in this volume, "Optical Effects," p. 142.

detail and dark ground lies in the fact that thus the subject attains greater brilliancy. One must refrain from making the detail of the subject too fine or delicate, for otherwise it becomes confused and will not carry. It is proper to use this method in the case of sculptured details, etc., which have a different tonality from their ground. The reason is evident since the first plane will always receive the greatest amount of light; to darken it artificially would be to negative the effect of the relief.

The advantage of adopting the dark detail and light ground is that such an arrangement is always more easy to comprehend or read. To be convinced one need only remember how much more legible and agreeable is dark printing on a white page than white printing on a black page. The Persians were noted advoates of the dark detail or subject. One also sees examples of it in the Italian "sgraffito" work, where a coat of a white wash was put on the house, over a dark coat of paint, and the design scraped through the outer covering, to the black one beneath. In designs for wall paper, where great brilliancy of subject is not desirable, where a decoration which will not absorb too much of the light of the room is needful, and confusion and illegibility are to be avoided, the dark subject and light ground are especially acceptable.

Other schemes for elucidating a subject when both it and the ground are of nearly the same intensity are the white border line and the black border line. Later, in studying "optical effects," we shall learn that whenever a contrast in successive spaces of dark and light is accentuated certain spaces tend to appear narrower (see page 143). When the subject is lighter than the ground, the white border line, while accentuating the contrast, makes the motive count to the extreme edge; so, if the line is not too white in contrast to the general tone of the design, the motive is not diminished in size. If the subject is darker than the background it might appear somewhat smaller than before the introduction of the border. The disadvantage of the use of the white border is that it often takes to itself the main interest of the design, and instead of seeing a beautiful flower or figure, the beholder notices only a tortuous and aggressive line.

In using the black border line, the subject, if lighter than the ground, almost invariably seems decreased in size. If it is darker than the ground it is merely strengthened. The black border line is a much safer expedient than the white line, as it has not the same tendency to assert itself.

Sometimes the contrast between the subject and background is too strong, and in order to lessen the existing harshness, a border or network of an intermediate intensity is introduced. By recourse to small details, breaking up the edge of an excessively dark background, the same result may be attained. Examples of this are the Gothic open-work ridge and crockets, which prevent the roofs and spires from cutting into the sky in too abrupt a manner; the Transition and French Renaissance dormers and decorated chimneys, such as one sees in charming profusion at Josselyn, Chambord, Blois and other chateaux of the period; and last of all, our modern crenellated parapets, however illogical and mistaken as a reversion to an effete mode of baronial defence, still are an evidence of an æsthetic and highly laudable desire for a less barren line and a more subtle contrast.

In studying the question of relative sizes of subjects and backgrounds, we may call to mind that two elements in the same composition should only be of equal size when they exactly repeat each other; in other words, in a piece of decoration either the subject or the ground should be decidedly the larger.

When the motive predominates the effect is rich and broad, but it may become heavy; and care must be exercised that good scale is retained. The Louis XIV. rinceau shows this tendency to heaviness, as does much modern work; we have spoken of the detail of the Paris Opera House, where so much genius is accompanied by the fault of overcharging ornament.

When the ground predominates, decoration becomes fine and elegant, but may easily be thin and weak. Herein lies a fault of much of our American work, where the puerile designer, not having studied enough to learn the motives of preceding ages, and without genius which might help him to invent something of his own, takes refuge in a scanty list of the most banal arrangements. His choice is usually a meager garland, which he strings out, in empty frieze decoration, believing meanwhile that such paucity of idea is or may pass for "refinement" and "restraint."

The best examples of delicate decoration are to be found in the Pompeian work, on the Greek vases, etc., of our museums, in the early Italian and French Renaissance, and in some Louis XVI. decorations. The Empire styles, which succeeded Louis XVI. time, tend toward the priggish meagerness and impotence of the modern designs just decried.

It is possible to consider the ground as being in itself a motive, rather than a certan amount of left-over space. The Byzantine decorations show attempts in this direction; and the Arabs went even farther, conceiving designs where the ground and subject alike had the same form, one fitting into the other (Fig. 40). In such a case, if there is great difference

FIG. 40.

in value between the two tones, the darker should be slightly larger than the lighter. Boulle, one of the Louis XIV. artists, composed his inlaid metal decorations in furniture design with a like skill. Here the metal runs out into the wood; first as a ground to set off the design of the wood, finally becoming the subject itself (Fig. 41).

Before abandoning the discussion of decoration pure and simple, let us add that the artist should supply his work with interesting suggestions; variety in idea, as well as in form, will give his designs life and color. Knowing how absolutely necessary are contrasts of motive, repetitions of any subject once fully expressed must be avoided. In the delineation of individual motives, wherever the character of the subject makes it possible, differences of weight and projection should

FIG. 41.

relieve the monotony which a more regular, perhaps more clumsy interpretation would offer. A careful study of Renaissance sprays and banderolles, so plenti- fully to be found as decorations of panels, etc., es- pecially a thoughtful examination of the earlier Italian

Renaissance examples, where flowers and other important motives, in higher relief, are united by tendrils,
delicately half embedded in the background, will be
the best mode of gaining a true conception of the sentiment which must pervade really artistic work. In
thus reverting to the masterpieces of the past, an artist
may make a useful comparison, noting that however
beautiful the French Francis I. bas-relief decorations,
they are far surpassed by their prototypes, the characteristic of the former being a rather too uniform
height of projection, while the latter have the subtle
play of light and shade the most faultfinding critic
or ardent lover of art could ask.

3. *The Application of Decoration to Form*

The general rule for the adaptation of decoration to a
particular form is that the decoration shall harmonize,
in character and arrangement, with the form. Thus,
in the choice of our decorative motives, we should not
only consult the ultimate use, etc., of the object, but
should select elements which can easily be placed upon
the shape in hand. Sometimes a simple form leaves
the artist more or less free, and he may then choose
one of two possible general schemes.

In certain cases, it may be suitable to make a design
covering the whole surface, without definite division;
in others, better to divide the surface into several
smaller spaces, each, of course, relating to its neighbor, and possibly to a central subject, but still quite
distinct and even complete in its own dominion.

As an example: for one elevation, it may be wise to

embrace the whole height of several stories, in a single order, as the Louis XIV. architects were prone to do, while in a second, the artist may properly follow the Italian or Francis I. scheme, and mark each floor level by a dividing course of mouldings, effectually cutting the façade up into superposed horizontal bands. The former of these, being the more concentrated, usually gives the greater decorative effect; but the second may still have decided charm, for the sake of scale, etc., may be advisable in large compositions, and should always be used where a logical reason for its adoption can be advanced.[1]

When considering the form only of decorative motives we divided them into two categories — those of two dimensions and those of three dimensions. In the same order, we shall take up the application of decoration to form.

(a) Keeping our general rule in mind, we conclude that if the silhouette, or other characteristic feature of a plane form, offer certain peculiarities the decoration should recognize them. When divisions are used they must follow the lead of the dominant lines of the primary form. In a façade, divisions will usually be horizontal or vertical. If an arch or curve is introduced, the axes would be horizontal and vertical. Only in a staircase, or other such aggressive construction — the octagonal staircase at Blois, for instance — would an inclined line be introduced. For a flat hori-

---

[1] It seems most illogical to make a façade, like that of the colonnade of the Louvre, which had no relation with the construction behind it.

zontal decoration the silhouette would probably determine a more intricate arrangement.

The principal lines of the silhouette, etc., still indicating the direction of the dividing lines of the decoration, we should have, as in Fig. 42, a peculiar

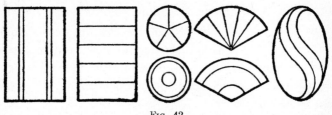

Fig. 42.

arrangement for each particular form. Especially in a vertical circle or oval should care be exercised that the vertical design, necessarily more or less free in this case, harmonize in detail with the curved silhouette.

An exception, in cases of very simple outlines, may be the use of obliques or spirals. The obliques, however, rigidly parallel, should, of course, not make too weak an angle with the contour, and the spirals should have a center in common with the silhouette. Moreover, toward the outer edge, the spirals should either make a strong angle with the silhouette or should become tangent to it.

(b) Again, we refer to our general rule and examine the form at our disposal, seeking to discover the dominant scheme of the modeling. If the object presents an axis of symmetry, our decoration should conform to the same axis; if the object presents a definite tend-

I

ency in a certain direction, our decoration should exhibit a like tendency (Fig. 43).

Thus, as we noted in the discussion of scale (page 64), we even find an exception to the rule forbidding

Fig. 43.

the smaller repetition of an element in the graduated ornament proper if the form diminishes in width or size. One sees this on certain vases, etc. (Fig. 44). Such a decoration seems to act as a support for the object. Other examples of graduated decoration are seen in the classical caissons of domes, etc.

When divisions are used, the generatrices of the surface should determine the directions of the divisions (Fig. 45, *a* and *b*); otherwise the decoration, sanely conceived from one point of view, becomes distorted as it follows the foreign law to which the form adheres. A glance at *c* of Fig. 45 will show this. In Fig. 45, *d*, the principal line, a human figure, would naturally be

straight in space, and so is badly chosen to follow the
distorted form of the vase.   Nevertheless, in elevation
it seems suitable enough.

FIG. 44.

This is an exceedingly easy rule to apply, yet it
is continually disregarded in practice.   When decorating the interior of a dome or coved surface,
how many artists have made the mistake of using

FIG. 45.

curves, circles, obliques, octagons, etc., imagining that
because they seemed to fall into place in the crude
sketch they would appear quite as well executed.

Fig. 46 shows a cove thus wrongly treated. The circles, seen at an angle, take the shape of lima-beans; the symmetrical octagons become distorted agglomera-

FIG. 46.

tions of curved lines, and the whole loses any claim to beauty.

Small circles and very short obliques may sometimes be used, because limited portions of the surface of a large dome approximate a plane; but dominating lines should always be parallel or perpendicular to the generatrices. When a dome is spherical, cylinders whose axes pass through the center of the sphere make an admissible intersection.

As with forms of two dimensions, the only real exceptions to these rules are for obliques, all rigidly parallel, or for spirals having a center in common with the underlying surface. Even with these restrictions the result is not usually very happy; the oblique lines tend to make the decoration appear twisted and out of plumb. Nevertheless, certain Chinese vases and baroque Renaissance columns present what might be called a solution.

Perhaps the best illustrations of the proper application of decoration to form are to be found in the
Greek or classical sculptured mouldings. Fig. 47

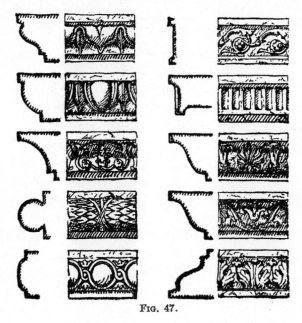

FIG. 47.

shows a set of these, and on examination one notes
how appropriate each design is to the corresponding
underlying form.

CHAPTER II

Optical Effects

As remarked, within certain limits the appearance of an object is a variable quantity. The piece of decoration, so rich and full of interest against a simple background, looks weak and insipid surrounded by a more virile design.

In such measure as the brilliancy of one composition may assert itself over and destroy that of its neighbor, aggressive qualities of one line may create a contrast detrimental to lines with which it is in juxtaposition. In other words, because a line is really straight, it does not at all follow that it must look so (Fig. 48, *b*).

The principle here involved is a wide-reaching one, and we should do wrong not to recognize, master and turn to account so important a factor in design. In so doing — in making our lines crooked, perhaps, that they may appear straight — although a deception seems involved, we are really more honest than we know. For we are thus asserting the great truth, namely, what is needful in art is that which will satisfy the human perceptions, not a mathematically determined conglomeration of lines or forms. It is here that the hopeful artist often goes astray, merely because he wishes to do what is considered correct, imagining that

118

a picture of a certain thing or an adherence to definite rules will be required of him. The old Greeks knew better when they gave ideal proportions to their statues and curved the lines of their temples.

The different categories into which the study of optical effects might be divided are so bound up, one within the other, that it seems unwise to attempt to delineate hard and fast cases. For the sake of some fealty to method, however, we shall consider: first, the optical effects of line; second, those of value; third, those of color; fourth, those of contrast in design. Also, we may distinguish the effects which exist as characteristic of peculiar arrangements and those which appear as a result of the special position of an object or point from which it is seen.

Different psychologists have advanced different theories to explain these illusions. Titchener, whom we shall cite in the following pages, follows Wundt's theory in general, *i.e.*,[1] that the illusions are "matters of perception, not of judgment." However, he adds on the same page that in reality many illusions are "'the resultant of several simultaneous tendencies' (Sanford) and that Wundt's principles ought, accordingly, to be supplemented by others." In any event, what is pertinent to the artist is not the reason, but the result.

When two straight lines come together or cross at

[1] Titchener, "Experimental Psychology," New York, Macmillan, 1901, Vol. I., Part I., p. 152. Here it may be well to say that a very complete list of the writings on this most interesting subject, Optical Illusions, is to be found in Mr. Titchener's "Experimental Psychology," Vol. I., Part II., pp. 305–309.

an angle of less than 90° the acute angle between them appears slightly greater than is really the case. In other words, the angle of two converging straight lines tends in appearance toward the right angle. The more acute the angle the more this tendency is exaggerated. If one line is more definite — blacker, broader, or in any way more visible — than the other, it is the less affected of the two.

Titchener expresses this as follows:[1] "The general formula is that small angles . . . are overestimated and obtuse angles underestimated in comparison with them."

There are many interesting results of this optical illusion. If (Fig. 48, a and b) we alternate the direc-

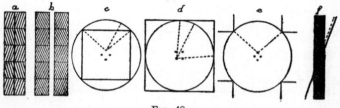

FIG. 48.

tion of sets of parallel lines, the straight line which makes an acute angle with them appears crooked. Two parallel lines (Fig. 48, b) seem successively to converge and diverge if contrasted with sets of parallels opposite in direction to each other.[2]

When a curve meets or is crossed by a straight line the same tendencies are exhibited by curve and line,

[1] "Experimental Psychology," Vol. I., Part II., p. 315.
[2] See Helmholtz, "Physiologischen Optik," Leipzig, 1867, pp. 565–566.

i.e., the directions of the line and of the tangent to the curve at the point of intersection seems slightly changed.[1] An immediate result of the last is that a circle, circumscribing, or circumscribed by a square, looks as though it were composed of four arcs with different centers (Fig. 48, *c* and *d*). Probably in *c* the definite angles of the square placed in contrast to the curve accentuate this effect and so make the circle look even flatter at the points where they touch it; the more so as, when the angles become exterior angles (*e* of Fig. 48), one notices the same flatness, while the curve might be expected to respond to the straight lines nearest it and become, on the contrary, more round.

If a flat arc of a circle is crossed in two points by a straight line, the line seems curved away from the arc. A result of this (even when line and curve stop a little short of the points of intersection) is the disagreeable aspect which a square-headed window presents when contrasted with a segmental, constructional arch above it. The flat lintel seems to curve in the opposite direction and apparently sags as though the weight were still too much for it. The remedy is the slight curving up of the under side of the lintel.

Helmholtz notes, in the "Physiologischen Optik," [2] that if one draws an angle of between 30° and 45°, one of whose sides is horizontal, and then through the summit draws a third, more vertical, line, forming a second angle with the inclined side of the first angle, so that the second angle will in appearance equal the first, one

[1] See Helmholtz, "Physiologischen Optik," p. 569.
[2] P. 546.

always, in reality, makes the second larger than the first. From this he explains the reason why the angle at the apex of an equilateral triangle, one of whose side is horizontal, appears more acute than the angles at the base.[1]

The following is another curious phenomenon of lines which cross:[2] When a light line crosses a broad band, making an acute angle with it, the two pieces of the lighter line must really be parallels in order to appear the continuation one of the other. The points where these two pieces touch the band would lie in a line making a slightly greater angle with the sides of the band than do the two pieces themselves (Fig. 48, f).

A peculiar effect is noticed when one looks, with one eye only, at a perpendicular erected on the middle of a horizontal. If the right eye is used (the eye should fix the point of intersection of the lines) the angle to the right of the perpendicular seems obtuse and the angle on the left acute. With the left eye, the phenomenon is reversed. If the vertical is continued below the horizontal, the lower left-hand angle seems too large to the right eye, etc.[3]

We have already seen how parallel lines may simulate convergents when under the influence of other convergents. Parallel lines also exhibit, in peculiar measure, the vagaries of the straight line whose image is not in the center of the field of vision. Lean over a table (Fig. 49) (it should be black and not shiny by

[1] "Physiologischen Optik," pp. 546–547.
[2] See the "Physiologischen Optik," p. 546.
[3] See the "Physiologischen Optik," p. 564.

preference) and place three pieces of paper upon it;
the first, A, in the center of the field of vision; the
other two, B and C, as far off in the outer portions of
the field as is compatible with their being seen distinctly without moving the eye. Then, still looking
fixedly at the central white paper, A, try to dispose a
fourth, D, between B and C, so that B, D and C may
lie in a straight line. Almost
invariably the paper D is
placed too near the center of
the field of vision, making B,
D, C curve in toward A.
Helmholtz assimilates these
curves to hyperbola.[1] The
distortion just noted is due in
large measure to the spherical
aberration of the eye itself, and
if B, D, C were really straight
it would appear to curve out.

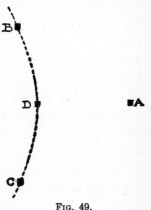

FIG. 49.

If, then, we have two parallel lines and the eye is at-
tracted toward a point between them, it might be possible to produce an agreeable effect by curving them
very slightly in at the center.

It is possible that some of the curves apparently used
by the Greeks in place of straight lines in their larger
temples — the Parthenon, for instance — presumably
intended to correct unpleasant optical effects, were, in
essence, the outcome of the illusion just described.[2]

---

[1] See "Physiologischen Optik," pp. 465 and 551–554.
[2] Many authorities are unwilling to accept the theory of an original or intentional curving of the lines of the Parthenon, although

Passing from straight lines, let us examine curves, and more especially circles or the arcs of circles. We need only pause to remark that the ordinary method of attempting to compose a curved line of short arcs of circles is not only inartistic, but, usually, quite unsuccessful. Unless a curve of the second degree is used — and then it should be geometrically constructed — all free curves ought to be drawn in free hand. Any empirical rule for the perpetration of a composed curve is sure to lead to ugly "breaks" in the line. The most that can be admitted is that the desired line be carefully studied and drawn in free hand and that a compass be used only at the very last, when a sufficient number of centers are tentatively found to allow of the different arcs practically covering the free-hand curve.

The pistolet, or French curve, is a makeshift, less successful than the compass.

If we try to judge by eye the amount of curvature 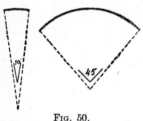 of an arc we may generally accept as a fact that, the shorter the arc — the less number of degrees by which it is measured — the flatter (than its real curvature) it looks. In other words, of two arcs, one measured by an angle of 10° and the other by an angle of 45°, but both described with the same radius, the former

FIG. 50.

they may admit something of the sort in other Greek temples. See "Die Baustile," zweiter theil, Die Baukunst der Griechen, by Dr. Josef Durm, Darmstadt, 1892, pp. 168–179. Also see Penrose's description of the Parthenon, etc.

will seem to have been described with a greater radius
than the latter (Fig. 50).

This is undoubtedly one reason why parallel or concentric curves cut, and thus, terminated by straight
lines, or even by other curves, so that they are measured by unequal angles, seem to be excentric, the
curve measured by the smaller angle having its radius
apparently lengthened (Fig. 51, *a* and *b*). A greater
cause for the last mentioned effect, at least as far as *a*
of Fig. 51 is concerned, probably lies in the fact that
the eye, in judging the width of the curved space between the concentric curves, tends at their ends to
measure from the end of one line to that of the other,
while in the middle of the curves it travels — as it

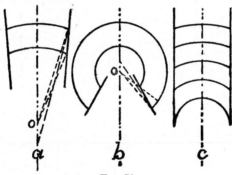

FIG. 51.

rightly should — along the normals to the curves.
Thus the curves look wider apart at their ends than in
the middle (Fig. 51, *c*).

If the secant lines are heavily drawn in, they themselves will somewhat affect the directions of the
curves. This influence, however, is much less power-

ful than that emanating from the two causes previously noted.

In the common architectural arrangement of Fig. 52 the outer circles *A* and *B* should not be drawn from the same centers as the inner ones at *C*. Since the angles which measure *A* and *B* are smaller that the

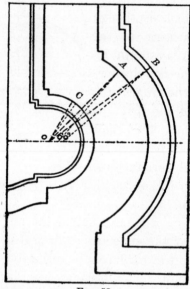

Fig. 52.

angle which measured *C*, the radii *A0'* and *B0''* should, in order to make the curves look concentric, be shortened and the centers 0' and 0'' placed farther out than 0.

It may be worth while to pause for a moment to examine some of the geometrical laws that govern the displacing of the centers of successive arcs of circles which, although limited by secant lines, we yet wish to have seem concentric. We shall analyze only usual cases where the secants are equidistant from the geometrical center of the figure, and thus admit of an axis of symmetry.

Instead of considering the length of radius (BO', Fig. 53) necessary to make a first arc, BC, measured by a smaller angle than a second, A, look as though it were concentric to the second, we may begin by examining the new inclination, which the tangent BI, at the end of the first arc, must assume. We shall call the angle α between the tangents of the original and corrected arcs the "angle of correction."

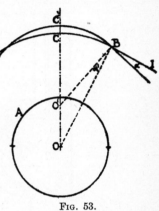

FIG. 53.

This angle α will be equal to the angle α' between the normals of the same arcs — from B to their centers.

The amount of curvature in successive circles drawn from a common center becomes less as the radius increases. A short arc, drawn with a radius of infinite length, may be considered a straight line.

Inasmuch as, in correcting successive concentric arcs which have been limited in a peculiar manner, we are trying to regain the effect which the complete circles would produce, we readily see that each corrected arc, as it recedes from the center, must be successively flatter than its predecessor, and that the last angle of correction can thus not exceed a certain limit.

Let us take a definite example of concentric arcs limited by straight secant lines (Fig. 54), the secants being inclined to each other so that their point of intersection will not fall between the center 0 and any of the arcs under consideration. (If the point of intersection of the secants lay between the center 0 and the arcs,

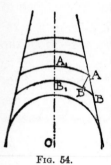

FIG. 54.

as in Fig. 51, *b*, the tendency of the angle of correction to increase as the radius increases, and of which we are about to speak, would merely be reversed.)

We have said that, in general, the two principal causes for the need of correction exhibited by the outer arcs lie, first, in the fact that they are measured successively by smaller angles, and second, in the fact that the distance between the ends of any two arcs along the secant (as from A to B) is longer than the distance along their normal (from A to B' or from A_1 to B_1). This is progressively true, from the circle which is tangent to the secants, up to the point where the secants converge, when it is reversed. If the secants were parallel or divergent it would, naturally, be true to infinity. Both the angles which measure the arcs, however, and the proportions between the secant and normal inter-arc distances decrease less and less rapidly as the arcs recede from the center.

We may therefore conclude that the successive angles of correction, which depend on the relations just analyzed, must progress from zero, at the tangent to the secants (for the tangent circle being complete needs no correction), to a certain greatest value, which greatest value if the secants are convergent, will be at their point of intersection: while if they are parallel or divergent it will be at infinity. Moreover, this maximum at infinity will be the amount of correction which the arc at infinity (whose radius in the case of parallel secants may be considered parallel to the secants) would need to make it appear to come from the general center.

We may also further conclude that the ratio of increase of the angles is a continually decreasing ratio, the rate of increase being maximum at the circle tangent to the secants and zero at infinity.

We have said that the maximum angle of the correction for arcs between parallels and divergents is at infinity. This maximum is variable in the cases of secants differently placed as regards the center.

The farther the secant is from the center, or, in other words, the longer the radius of the circle tangent to the secants, the greater is the difference between the distance from a given point on the secant, to the point of tangency, and the distance from the same point, along a normal of the circle, to the point where the normal cuts the circle. This difference, with the point at infinity, is equal to the radius of the tangent circle; and as it is just this difference which is one of the two causes of the need for correction of the arc at infinity, we see that the greater the distance of the secant from the center, the greater will be the angle of correction. (The radius of the tangent circle being

K

finite, the maximum of comparison between the arcs is constant, 180°–0°.)

We have also noted that the greater the angle by which an arc is measured, the more readily is the center placed and the less need is there for correction. Moreover, this need entirely disappears when the circle is complete and exists only slightly for the half circle, while it is maximum when the arc is reduced to a single point. Evidently, in our present problem, only convergent secants will give us an arc which is reduced to a point. Parallel secants, however, give us a limited

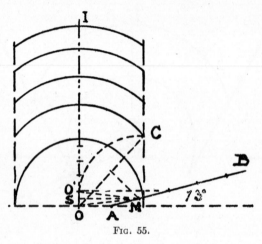

FIG. 55.

arc at infinity; and we further conclude that the greater the angle of divergent secants, the smaller will be the maximum angle of correction.

Fig. 55 is a simple approximate geometrical construction for the correction of arcs between parallels. For a tangent circle with a radius of $0^m.0175$, and with parallel secants the maximum angle of correction is about 15°.

The line AB is drawn from the point A (A is situated on a perpendicular to the secant which passes through the center of the tangent circle and is halfway between the center and the point where this perpendicular cuts the tangent circle) to make an angle somewhat smaller than the maximum angle of correction, say 13°, with the perpendicular to the secants or to the axis oI.

We wish to draw a corrected circle from C on the secant BC.

Join C and o, and on the middle of Co erect a perpendicular which will cut AB in a point M. From

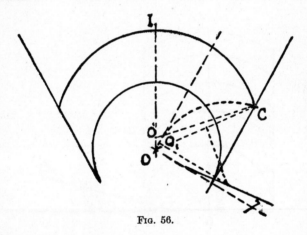

Fig. 56.

M as a center, with Mo as a radius, describe an arc, $oo'C$, which will cut the axis oI in o'. This point o' is the center for the corrected arc to pass through c and be limited by the parallels. We may deduce a more exact placing of o', if we note that a perpendicular, from M to the axis, will cut the axis halfway between o and o'. The angle oCo' between the two radii oC and

$o'C$ will be equal to the angel SMo, and therefore equal to MoA. As M is taken farther out on AB, which means, as c is taken farther out on the secant, the angle MoA tends nearer to the maximum.

AB should, theoretically, be a curve, beginning at A and tending to become a straight line, making the maximum angle of correction (here 15°) with oA.

In the case of divergents, a parallel to one of the secants is drawn through the center o (Fig. 56) and the foregoing construction again carried out. The

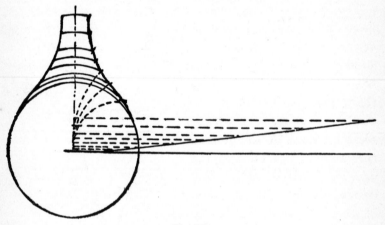

Fig. 57.

point o_1 corresponding to the center o' of Fig. 55 is joined to C, Co_1 being produced until it cuts the axis oI in o', thus giving the center for the corrected arc at C between the divergents in question. The maximum angle is, in the present case, reduced by the considerable divergence of the secants to about 8°.

Fig. 57 shows a construction where a constant radius

is used, the length of the arcs being so limited that they seem concentric. The same principle of construction is adopted as in the foregoing problem, the maximum angle of correction being about 8°. The curved lines which are the loci of the ends of the curves tend, at infinity, to become parallel. The maximum angle of correction should be the same as that which these parallels would require. It is the zero point which is displaced.

The foregoing analysis has not been given with the intention of inducing the designer to use a geometrical construction in correcting concentric arcs, but merely to show what elements, in the disposition of the arcs, will increase or decrease the need of correction. Inasmuch as the drawing in of the secants in a design, as well as the presence of other lines, would materially alter the amount of correction needed, it would be futile to attempt anything like a mathematical construction. What

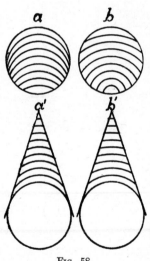

Fig. 58.

is to be aimed at is an agreeable effect; and this being true, the taste of the cultured artist must be its creator.

Fig. 58 shows how arcs of circles, under certain circumstances, may seem quite other than what they really are; *a* and *a'* are circles of constant radius and *b* and *b'* are circles from common centers. In *a* the

lower arcs look flatter than the upper ones, while in a'
they seem almost concentric. In b the upper arcs
seem too flat, while in b' they all need some correction.

In regard to half circles which are terminated by
a normal (as in the niche in plan, Fig. 59, a), the curve
always seems less than its proper length, unless a short
straight line is added; in other words, unless the center
is slightly stilted. Such a form as that of Fig. 59, c,

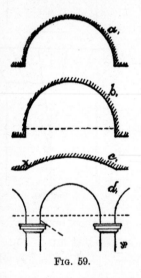

FIG. 59.

should never be used; the angle
at x is a weak one (see pages 45
and 46). In the elevation of an
arcade, or arch, with impost
mouldings, the arc should be even
more stilted than would otherwise be necessary, as, the beholder being almost invariably
below the line of the center, the
projection of the mouldings cuts
off part of the stilting.

Passing from the question of
arcs, we examine illusions which
result when lines radiating from a
center are crossed by straight lines.

One secant line seems curved away from the center,
because of the overestimation of the acute angles.

Two parallel secants placed on both sides of the center
also seem bowed around it.

Of parallel secants on the same side of the center,
the ones nearest the center seem much more curved
about it than do the outer ones. In certain cases, some
observers see the secant farthest out bend in at the

middle. When the problem takes the form of Fig. 60, *A*, the outer secant definitely bends down or in toward the center, especially when the lower secant and two verticals are blacker, or the space, here representing the window opening, is darkened. This is mainly because the eye measures the distance between the secants, along the radiating lines; since those inclined are longer than the more perpendicular ones, the secants seem farther apart at the ends.

Another illusion of Fig. 60, *A*, interesting to architects, is that the radiating lines do not seem to have the same center. For those toward the middle, the center recedes: this in spite of the tendency of the acute angles toward the extremities to make the inclined lines appear less so. It is probably due to measuring the distances between the secants along inclined lines. Finding these less perpendicular to the secants than expected, we

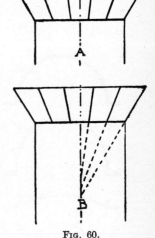

FIG. 60.

judge their centers of radiation too far up. Fig. 60, *B*, shows the proper manner to correct this illusion when designing a flat arch. The joints of the voussoirs tend toward the perpendicular at their ends; but this is very slight and does not need correction. Spacing is done on the intrados to avoid diminishing the keystone.

We have already spoken of the apparent distortion

which the spiral gives to forms, and the care with which it should be used. Indeed, a disagreeable sensation that the figure is revolving is often the result of the use of spirals and similar figures centering in a point.

All dominant lines introduced into a definite contour tend to alter the apparent shape of the figure. Parallel divisions of marked contrast of value are perhaps the most potent agents in producing such distortions.

There are two opposite causes acting upon figures which show divisions. In the first place : of two equal spaces, one divided by regular and impersonal lines or bands and the other counting without divisions, in its whole length, the divided space appears the longer. Helmholtz gives four examples of this,[1] as reproduced in Fig. 61, *A*, *B*, *C* and *D*. In *A*, as a better manner of showing the principle, *ab* and *bc* are made to look equal, *bc* having divisions across it. Measurement proves *ab* the longer. In *B*, *a* seems taller than it is wide, while *b* seems wider than it is high. In *C*, angles 3 and 4 seem obtuse and 1 and 2 acute. In the equilateral triangles of *D* the angle at the apex of *a* seems very much too acute, while the summit of *b* is thrown to the right. Helmholtz adds that an empty room looks smaller than a furnished one ; a figured wall, larger than a plain one, and that ladies' dresses with horizontal stripes make the figure appear taller — "Damenkleider mit Querstrichen lassen die Figur höher erscheinen."

[1] "Physiologischen Optik," p. 563.

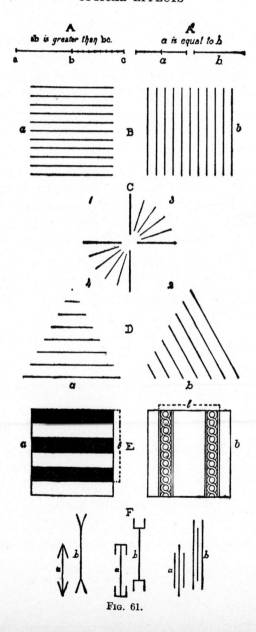

FIG. 61.

The only trouble is that experience does not always carry this out. It would be almost impossible to induce either a stout woman or her dressmaker to put horizontal stripes, instead of vertical ones, on the dress which is to reduce the appearance of fatness. Moreover, the usual trick for making a room seem high is to put vertical stripes on the wall from top to bottom.

An explanation is to be found in Fig. 61, E. Here, at a first glance, a seems broader than it is high and b higher than it is wide. The fact that the divisions take on an importance of their own and thus induce the observer to ignore that portion of the figure which lies outside of the limit set by them (marked by l in both figures), tends to make the design an apparent confutation of Helmholtz's theory. It is only when the observer has taken careful cognizance of the whole figure that the anticipated, previously noted effect tardily asserts itself.

Titchener,[1] following Wundt, gives the psychophysical explanation of the foregoing. He says that we estimate such distances as that of Fig. 61, A, by eye movements. In such figures as 61, A', the eye is arrested by the middle division of a, the tendency is to take in the line as a whole by a single fixation, and a, really equal to b, seems the shorter. On the next page Titchener gives Wundt's law for this: "Distances, the traversing of which requires a movement of regard that is interrupted by fixation-points or prescribed by fixation-lines, appear longer than

[1] "Experimental Psychology," Vol. I., Part II., p. 313.

distances that can be traversed without fixation-points or in complete freedom, without prescription of path."

Therefore, if two striking vertical bands are made from top to bottom of a skirt, it will seem longer than otherwise. Also, if bands go from floor to ceiling of a room, the eye does not interest itself in the horizontal direction, follows them in the vertical, and the whole height counts. Probably if impersonal, therefore regular, divisions could be made in the length of the bands, the height would be further increased.

Another example of illusions of extent cited by Titchener [1] is the Müller-Lyer illusion (Fig. 61, *F*— in all three cases the middle line of *b* seems longer than that of *a*). Wundt's law [2] is as follows: "A distance which, in virtue of its fixation-lines, offers a motive to the continuance of movement in the same direction is adjudged greater, and a distance which in virtue of similar lines in opposite direction offers a motive to the inhibition of movement is adjudged less, than an objectively equal distance in the traversing of which such motives are not operative."

The illusions of Oppel, Delbœuf and Kundt can be seen in a figure composed of a vertical and horizontal line, equal in length and crossing through the middle point of each.[3] "In binocular vision the vertical line appears longer than the horizontal (Oppel), and the upper vertical limb appears longer than the lower

[1] "Experimental Psychology," Vol. I., Part I., p. 159.
[2] *Ibid.*, Vol. I., Part II., p. 314.
[3] *Ibid.*, Vol. I., Part II., p. 315.

(Delbœuf). In monocular vision the outer horizontal limb appears longer than the inner (Kundt)."

As a result of the foregoing, if one wishes a square to look square the interior decoration must be conceived (as is the square itself), with regard to two like axes of composition, perpendicular to the sides of the figure. The illusion of Oppel might induce us to

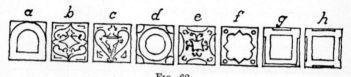

FIG. 62.

slightly lessen the height of the whole. In Fig. 62, *a*, *b*, *c* and *g*, are faulty examples, while *d*, *e*, *f* and *h* are good. Especially in a repeated motive or suite should the principle of composition remain the same; and we may go even farther and say that the main dividing lines must inclose elements where the shape and actual size balance each other, values being approximately maintained.

This question of contrasts of value is most important. Usually the greater the contrast the greater is the personality of a division. But two other factors, of irradiation in the eye and of diffusion of the light rays, cause definite and dominant effects. Already, under "Backgrounds" (page 105), the apparent difference in size between a white detail on a black ground and an equally large black detail on a white ground was mentioned. This is noticeable in the squares of Fig. 63, *a*.[1] Moreover, if the accommodation of the

[1] See also Helmholtz, "Physiologischen Optik," p. 321.

eye becomes less exact the
black square diminishes
and the white one aug-
ments. Again, in equally
wide alternating black and
white bands the white, still
encroaching on the black,
seems the wider. Other
examples of the same are *b*
(Fig. 63), in which there
seems to be a white di-
agonal through the figure; *c*
(same figure), in which the
black bands broaden out as
they get lighter, and *d*, the
white bands broadening
out as they get lighter. In
c a curious blending of two
effects is seen; for, when
the figure is badly out of
focus, the total width of the
darker portion is much narrower than that of the portion where the bands do not
divide the width. In *d* this
is not true. The black here,
making a sharp contrast
all along the edge of the
figure, forces the divided
portion to count or suffer
equally with the undivided.

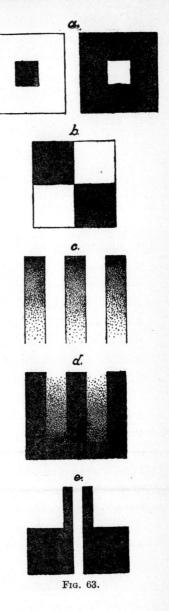

FIG. 63.

As suggested, these effects of contrast are due to irradiation and to the circles of diffusion of the points of light lapping over on the dark ground. A white space may seem diminished from the inverse of the latter cause, provided the black bands on either side of it are narrower than the diameter of the circles of diffusion caused by the faulty accommodation of the eye.[1] In Fig. 63, *e*, the white strip of the same width in all its height seems to have the form of an Indian club, while the narrow black strips of the upper part of the figure broaden out at the end.

In the indication of a "rendu" it is necessary to make small, light succeeding motives or spaces, such as balusters, etc., which count individually, much wider than they would be in nature. This is because the contrast between the value of the motives and the darker intervals between them is usually accentuated in the drawing; and the reduced size of the drawing allows of the width of the pictured interval being less than the width of the circles of diffusion where its width in execution would not. An additional important reason for augmenting the width of the motive and lessening that of the space is that the line of the drawing counts with the darker value, thus encroaching the more on the motive when once the rendering is finished. As it is almost impossible to avoid "running over the line" in a small scale "rendu," that also is to be forestalled. As a definite rule, in all drawings at or under a scale of one fourth of an inch to the foot, indicated stone balusters should touch

[1] "Physiologischen Optik," p. 326.

each other (Fig. 64); rendered and seen at a distance, they seem to be properly separated. The easiest manner of indication is to draw the holes instead of the balusters themselves. Indeed, similar tricks of indication may be invented for nearly all objects by simply drawing the masses that show most in the model, without reference to their meaning.

FIG. 64.

Narrow white bars in a rendered window must also be made wider than the scale would suggest. Later on, in studying indication of plan, allusion will be made to the influence of divisions on the apparent size of dimensions. Suffice, for the moment, to say that the reducing of certain spaces and the increasing of others by the introduction of judicious or injudicious mosaic may make or mar a plan. It is the abuse of this power over the appearance of things which has called down so many anathemas on the heads of the French architects of the modern school.

With regard to irradiation caused by a brilliant light [1] (although these phenomena are of less usual interest to the architect), if one holds a straight ruler so that the edge cuts across the flame of a candle the semblance of a nick is apparant in the ruler at the point where is the flame. Thus bars, seen with the sun directly behind, tend to disappear, etc. An accentuation of a similar effect is seen in the photograph of a tree with the sun shining through the leaves into the camera.

[1] See Helmholtz, "Physiologischen Optik," p. 322 and following.

When a triple division occurs and we wish each part to look exactly a third of the total width, the middle space should be very slightly larger than the two side ones (Fig. 65, *a* and *b*). In *b* the centers would usually be on the same horizontal line. That the keystone of the central arch is slightly reduced in height thereby is not noticeable. To retain a uniform keystone, the two side arches may be slightly over-stilted. Augmenting the central space of three is necessary, because we

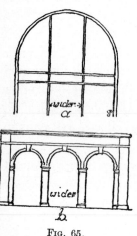

Fig. 65.

are so accustomed to seeing a definitely dominating motive on the axis, that when absolute equality exists the middle division looks undersized.

Another somewhat similar comparison of spaces appears in the desire to see the mat below a picture slightly wider than those on the other three sides (Fig. 66, *A*). Perspective may enter as an abetting factor. It certainly does in the exaggerated stilting, necessary to all bases and plinths, which are over projections and above the level of the

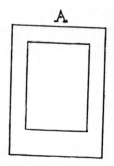

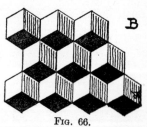

Fig. 66.

eye. In the excessive inclination which must be given to roofs and domes we see the influence of perspective. Of course, a practical reason for never making the top of a dome too flat is that rain and snow would otherwise accumulate there. Another distortion that results from perspective is the accentuation of the steepness of a pediment seen fore-shortened from the side.

Examples exist (that of the staircase of the Vatican) [1] with an accentuation of perspective attempted in the progressive shortening and drawing together of a vista of columns. This is not very advisable; it resembles too much the theatrical effects, well enough for stage scenery, but decidedly out of place and character in more serious decoration. As to the treatment of scenery itself, we may leave the discussion in the hands of the scene painter, merely noting that if the observer is displaced from the point of sight, not only does the decoration seem distorted, but an accurate judging of the real relation of lines and forms becomes impossible. In parallel perspectives this is easily attested. Here, although the lines are necessarily parallel, the expectation of the sensation which vanishing parallels in nature would give, i.e., the sensation given in the drawing by convergents makes them seem to be divergent. In picturings of circular forms, if arcs of circles are mistakenly substituted for the ellipses of projection, the arcs do not look like portions of circles.

An important chapter in the psychological study of optical illusions is that treating perspective illusions

[1] See Letarouilly, "Le Vatican," Librairies Imprimeries Réunies, Paris.

L

offered by simple geometrical diagrams. These are of lesser importance to the decorator, as his designs are usually definite as representations. Where the design is purely geometrical, perspective illusions are more or less out of keeping. Fig. 66, *B*, shows a faulty yet much used arrangement, ordinarily adopted for floor tiling. The impression of treading on the sharp points of projecting cubes is not agreeable.

If an arrangement, having in its composition spots or elements prominent enough to form a design of their own, be seen from one side so that the spots fall into lines other than those on which the original arrangement was formed, the general effect will be completely changed. This is noticeable in wall papers with small bunches of flowers arranged in a checkered pattern.

While speaking of the aspect of things we must refer (page 91) to the mistake of placing a symmetrical motive, such as a dome, over a triangular or pentangular plan. The designer ought to keep in mind that a monument, or other similar composition which silhouettes, if planned on a square, should be studied in diagonal, as well as in front elevation. Naturally, in all designs where relief exists, the perspective view, if not actually drawn out, should be continually kept in mind. Although a perspective drawing may be an aid, reliable help is only obtainable from a good model, or that still more expensive commodity, experience.

In arrangements of value and color much uncertainty exists for the designer, because of the difference in appearance of an element isolated, or contrasted with other elements. Thus the alteration of one part of a drawing might necessitate a complete change in all parts. This may be turned to account in many ways, as the following illustration will show. A well-known painter had finished a portrait, pronounced by relatives of the sitter (unusual in such cases) to be as good in likeness as it was excellent in the possession of those artistic qualities which always pervaded the works of the skilled technician. The inevitable "but," however, had to be brought in; the coloring was "a little too florid," they thought. The artist, wishing to gratify them, asked for a day's more work on the portrait; the result was pronounced perfect. The good critics imagined that the head had been largely re-painted : the artist knew he had but changed the background from green to a brown of the same value.

Contrasts of complementary colors accentuate each other, as do those of value, light and dark. Also, when two fields of color, complementary to each other, come together, each may be slightly altered (made whiter) along the edge by the continual movement of the eye, which movement causes the impression made by one color on the retina, to cover the edge of the neighboring field.[1]

The complementary colors as given by Helmholtz are :[2]

> red and greenish blue,
> orange and pure blue,
> yellow and indigo blue,
> greenish yellow and violet.

[1] Helmholtz, "Physiologischen Optik," p. 388 and following.
[2] *Ibid.*, p. 277.

Pure green has no direct complement. In mixing colored lights, however, green, violet and red form the three primary colors; in painting, red, yellow and blue are usually accepted as primaries.

Drawings and pictures of all sorts have to be made for the light in which and for the distance from which they are to be judged. This is one of the difficulties attending the making of both out-of-door sketches and studio work. In general, drawings for an exhibition should be particularly brilliant. To state succinctly what changes occur: *the greater the light by which a drawing or painting is to be seen the longer must be the scales, both of value and color.* That is to say, the greater the illumination, the darker should be the darkest value, and the lighter the lightest. With colors, there must be greater difference between those complementary to each other — less grayness of tone.

Despite the advisability of using a long scale, small black or white spots are rendered more apparent and disagreeable by increased lighting. The same cause makes work in a short key appear better in inadequate lighting than in an exhibition. While strong light seems to shorten the scales of value and color, possibly to accentuate the effect by increasing actual contrasts of light and shade in frames and other objects in the room, it also makes more definite, leaves less to the imagination, inaccurate and harsh contrasts. Of course, the longer the scale of value or color the better will the work "carry" to a distance.

Drawings in a uniformly high key can support strong light better than those in a uniformly low one; but either will be injured by the neighborhood of another drawing, conceived in a larger scale. Exception may be made for paintings which portray a definite effect. A landscape 'twixt darkness and dawn in a low key like those of M. Pointelin in the Luxembourg gallery, or a sunlight study like some of the impressionist paintings, high in key, gives the expected contrast with other work.

Even in such paintings as those of Mr. Whistler's or M. Eugène Carrière's, where the artist implies a particular effect, the picture is less likely to suffer after hanging. But when no peculiarity in the lighting of the model is shown (this is definitely the case in architectural rendering) a long scale should be adopted.

If a particular color exists in superabundance in the light by which a painting is seen, that color, with its complement, suffers in the painting. Inversely, a drawing made by candle-light and exhibited by day has almost invariably too much yellow, while the violets are crude. In the same way, a drawing made by the rays of the setting sun is likely to have faults in the red and green notes; a study by moonlight, to look green in the daytime.

This is probably because the color, like that of the light, seems white to the painter, and he must use a great deal of it in order to make an impression on his eye; the complement of this color, having a superabundance of colored rays to absorb, is made crude. As a result, the color which bears the same name as that of the light is likely, exhibited in daylight, to be too dark in value.

A further evidence of this is the power which sunlight has over colors. The most varied and barbaric conglomerations of color appear harmonious with sunshine on them. From this the architect and decorator may derive two important lessons : First, for exterior decoration only use great contrasts of color in southern countries, where strong sunlight prevails. Exterior work in all northern countries should be more or less uniform in tonality. The colors which predominate in the landscape under our colder climates accentuate the need of observing this rule. Second, although a cartoon for an interior decoration with strongly contrasting colors may seem attractive at a small scale, the reduced lighting which it is likely to receive when executed should induce the artist to shorten his color and value scales. He should keep the key high, rather than low, for large masses of dark color lessen the decorative effect and absorb the light of the room or hall. Another element, accentuating the need of keeping the colors together, is that the larger the fields of color, the less likely they are to fuse together in the way small neighboring spots do.

When decorating interior walls surfaces the color must be made much grayer and, for all deep colors, much lighter than seems desirable in a small sample.

Before leaving the discussion of optical effects, a word must be said in regard to some few dispositions of line to be avoided for æsthetic reasons.

Given an axis, a series of parallel obliques, or a running design composed upon a similar basis, should not continue around an interior, or as a frieze or girdle about

an exterior, without the direction of the obliques being
reversed at the axis. In any case, it is usually disagreeable to see a running band of obliques which has no
beginning or end ; the eye is distressed by the temptation to follow the design without stopping point.
Special arrangements ought to be studied for these be-
ginnings and endings.

Long inclined lines, such as those of the classic
pediments and Renaissance gables, should also have
a definite starting point. This the ancient and Renaissance artists realized when they terminated these
lines with an antefix or fineal. We may find the chief
necessity for such a vertical in the fact that, unsup-
plemented, the angle of the silhouette would be obtuse
and weak. In some cases prominent horizontals, a
gargoyle or projecting cornice may supplant the vertical.

CHAPTER III

Style [1]

APROPOS of the application to decoration of the technical laws of composition it may be well to speak of the influence exerted over that application by styles of earlier ages. Such remarks must, necessarily, be a matter of opinion. I should be sorry to have the following regarded as more than that.

As may be gathered from preceding pages (see "Unity of Style," page 47), it seems to me that any general application of an earlier style, the outcome of a civilization different from ours, is a mistake both of logic and taste. Such can only be acceptable when the special example is one in which our present ideas have retained the coloring of an earlier epoch. For a Roman Catholic cathedral, Gothic might still be an appropriate expression; yet in some other modern uses, absurd. As a result of modern civilization's markedly different expressions (in Germany, France, England and America), I believe that the architecture of each country should present national characteristics. However, for one who has lived — not traveled, but lived —

---

[1] An excellent review of the styles of the Christian era is to be found in M. Henry Havard's "Les Styles," Paris, Librairie Charles Delgrave. Indeed the whole series "Les Arts de l'ameublement" of which this volume forms a part will be of interest to the art student.

in these different countries, there disappears the great dissimilarity seemingly existent to the casual traveler.

One may fairly say that the Frenchman, German and American of the year 1900 more nearly resemble each other in their modern needs than the up-to-date American and his forefather, the old Colonialist of a hundred years ago. Moreover, the inter-race differences, still strongly noticeable in some matters, become less and less decided as facility of intercourse increases. It may be, in a few hundred years, the artistic expression in one part of the civilized world will be the counterpart of that in another.

Be this as it may, if the artist sincerely expresses what he feels, makes no vain attempt to generate a national style, but simply works for the best advantage of the requirements of his country and generation, the progress of art will take care of itself.

Adopting an earlier style, we ought fully to realize the aims of its creators. We should, then, save ourselves from falling into the kind of fault often committed nowadays by illiterate architects, who use Gothic without conceiving, in the vaguest way, what wonderful constructional principles underlie that most logical period of the world's architectural history.

If we work in a historical style, our adaptation should be pure and scholarly; but the expression of style must not detract from the character of the building. The visitor, shown the sights of a town, should never be tempted to exclaim: "What an excellent example of French Renaissance!" instead of, "What a successful design for a library!"

All architectural styles of civilized countries, from the classic to the modern, seem to me to have a possible relation with some phase of our present existence. Those of the Middle Ages, of a time when the religious sentiment was fully developed, are susceptible of being applied to similar edifices of the present day; those of the early Renaissance may well be adapted to modern domestic work, while the later French Renaissance of the Louis' is allied, in feeling, to much of what one finds in the present expression of society. But all of these applications are to be modified by the personality (naturally a present-day personality) of the architect.

In the first part of this volume it was suggested that the style which may become characteristic of the twentieth century will draw its individuality from a free and proper use of steel or of concrete. Certainly, present necessity for strength of construction, coupled with reduced points of support, is best met by unreserved recourse to such materials. In acknowledging a constructional principle, we shall be as well repaid as were the Gothic architects of former centuries. If we imagine a frank showing of the framework to be ugly, is it not because we have accustomed ourselves to another flavor in the preparation of our architectural dishes? Are we not somewhat like the young child who, having tasted nothing but milk, turns away from the meat which will give to it the strength of manhood?

Perhaps the greatest benefit which we may derive from preceding styles lies not so much in an application to modern decoration as in the refinement which their careful study is sure to impart (see again in Part I., page 38). By taking up first one style and working therein for some time, only leaving it for another when the finer qualities of the epoch have been appreciated and assimilated, the student becomes impressed with the more subtle traits of the masters of the past age; later, although abandoning forms and materials for which he has no use, he will retain the marks of a gentle breeding in art which communion with great geniuses cannot fail to produce.

PART IV

CHAPTER I

PRACTICAL SUGGESTIONS IN DESIGN APPLIED TO DECORATIVE WORK

WE recall that a first general law of all designs to be executed in a particular material is that these be in harmony with the material.

An architect has, usually, two or three materials to cope with, in even the simplest elevation. He should be careful that the line carried through by metal mouldings, although offering as broad a band of decoration as the stone, is, in the finer material, interpreted by a more delicate profile. This principle of decoration is so often ignored that too much can hardly be said in its behalf. When the composition is to occupy a particular place or position, the motives should be designed with a due regard to their placing (see page 34).

Keeping these laws in mind, we shall pass in review different materials in which decorative work is usually executed. This can only be done superficially, for each separate art would require a volume or several volumes to itself. It will, nevertheless, be possible to cite the characteristics inherent in each material, and this should be quite enough for our present need.

We shall first take up those materials which have prominent constructional qualities.

Stone, it is well known, resists best in compression. For this reason the stone arch is a better element of construction than the lintel. The design, to be carried out in stone, should not present elements which have to resist a shear or a bending moment.

Moreover, stone is a material which only resists when the section has a certain dimension, and fine or delicate fillets and shafts should be avoided. Such absurd tracery as that found in Henry VII. chapel in Westminster Abbey, and the decadent Gothic of Saint Maclou, at Rouen, are not examples to be imitated.

But it is not sufficient, in preoccupation about the material at hand, merely to assure ourselves that designs are stony in character. There are too great differences between the harder and rougher granites and the fine grained marbles to allow of such a gross grouping. It is almost as inappropriate to carve a detailed and delicately chased Corinthian capital out of brutal granite as to copy the choir stalls of Amiens cathedral in marble. If a stronger and rougher stone is needed, so also is a more robust design.

The fibrous composition of wood renders it eminently able to resist tension and, in somewhat less degree, compression, when these occur in line with the fibers; also compression, a shear, or the tendency to bend, when they are applied in a direction perpendicular to the line of the fibers.

The two most usual misuses of wood are giving it

a form which is in contradiction to its fibrous composition, and cutting out of it mouldings properly belonging to stone.   Inasmuch as the fibers of a piece of wood are naturally straight, we may accept as a law that all wood arches (except those composed of several thicknesses of plank, Fig. 67, *a*, in which case the fibers follow the direction of the curve) are unnatural and illogical (Fig. 67, *b*).   Even such a com-

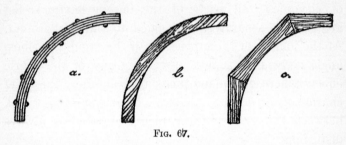

FIG. 67.

posed arch as that of *c* (Fig. 67) is to be avoided, if possible.   The arch does not belong to wood ; and, although the charm of the old English timber work is not to be denied, we can hardly fail to recognize how much more attractive are the examples where no irrational silhouettes are introduced.   Even in small compositions for furniture carving, etc., if any resistance is desired or implied, excessive curves should be set aside.   In cabinet work, as in carpentering, the true artist is never ashamed of a good joint.   Moreover, the frank accentuation of the constructive elements of any design is always reassuring, giving the observer a feeling of security.

Owing to the fact that wood shrinks in the direction perpendicular to that of the fibers, all joints in panel work, etc., should be covered by mouldings. It is also best to avoid broad panels, because they not only make the shrinkage at each joint greater, but are themselves more likely to crack. We should not depend on glue to hold a joint — it is a makeshift, and invariably breaks out in the end.

In wood carving, never stoop to the patchwork, so often affected by manufacturers, where, for the sake of cheapness, all parts of the design having relief are cut out separately and glued to the background. At the joining of these pieces with the ground, a sharp angle necessarily shows, preventing any of the subtle effects where one plane melts into another, the chief charm of a delicate design. Moreover, the break between the grains of the pieces of wood is always disturbing.

With wood, as with stone, we must adapt our designs to the especial species in hand. The finer carving, proper for walnut, rosewood, mahogany, ebony, etc., should take on a more vigorous cast when intended for oak; the softer woods should only be cut into broad silhouettes whose appearance will not be materially altered by blunting of the edges.

Above all, over-charged and minute work resembling that of ivory ought not to be indulged in. Although a delicate material, wood chips easily; even though it be sufficiently cared for to escape mishaps, the suggestion that projections may be fragile is enough to condemn the design.

Of late years much charming decoration in burnt wood has been executed; but usually for small objects only. The rich brown effects of burning might be used in a broader way in general interior work. Acid effects on wood, raising the grain in imitation of the Japanese rubbed wood surfaces, might also be utilized.

Iron is so various in its different guises that we shall study each one of them separately.

From a constructive point of view, steel and iron are the most serviceable materials known. They resist in the three directions and necessitate only a minimum section. When in an exposed position, they must always be protected by paint or galvanizing, etc., and if a fire-proof construction is desired, by terra-cotta, concrete or a similar insulator.

Cast-iron is often moulded in decorative design. The ease with which it is shaped tempts one to imitate the forms appertaining to other materials. The most usual transgressions come from the casting of iron capitals which have the large proportions and, at the same time, the fineness of detail of stone. For the first, the appearance of unnecessary waste of material is distressing. For the second, the paint which must cover iron work, together with the irregularities which result from the manner in which casting of this sort is done, render attempted delicate detail ungainly. A more blocked-out design, of lesser proportions, should be substituted for the everlasting distorted Corinthian capital and thick column.

Wrought and hammered iron open up to us a quite different field. Here the larger bars of iron, worked in the forge and supplemented by finer bars, with sheet iron hammered into leaves, etc., may make a composition of the greatest interest and variety. The old wrought iron work of the Florentines is full of a character and charm which cannot be outrivaled by the even more noted epochs of Louis XIV., XV. and XVI. In its simplicity it is eminently fitted to serve us as a means of inspiration for domestic compositions. Of the French styles, worthy examples are the Grilles at Nancy, some of the Versailles work, the Louis XIV. interior wrought iron or steel doors of the Galerie d'Apollon of the Louvre, and the charming designs of Blondel, Briseux and other Louis XV. and Louis XVI. artists.

Combinations of wrought iron, or even better, of polished steel and brass, may be used with great effect. The stronger constructive elements should be of steel; the lighter decorations of brass.

It may be well to note here that combinations of metal, such as iron and zinc or copper, should not be used in such a manner that an electric current might be established between them. Otherwise a corroding of the metals ensues and speedy destruction is the result.

Bronze is ordinarily only used for decorative purposes, and the finer and more careful casting, either in sand or by the wax process, allows of greater delicacy than that of iron. Hence, fine members of slight section are characteristic of bronze design. The ease with which bronze may be worked also permits of delicate chasing. This method of execution at times supplements casting. Excessive retouching is, however, inadvisable. The original model is

M

necessarily made without reference to such changes, and the tool lines seem sharp and out of place.

Bronze is nearly always finished with a patina, which should be rubbed off from the more salient points. This allows the metal underneath to show through and contrast with the outer tone. We see here the reason why copper, often substituted in America for the more expensive alloy, is so inferior to it.

It would be too long to cite the different styles where choice examples of bronze work are to be found. From the early days of Greece to our modern time, in Japan, indeed through all the East, as well as in Europe, we find beautiful evidences of the artist's skill in designing for this wonderfully adaptable material.

Tin and pewter show some of the characteristics which bronze presents. On account of their softness it is better not to chase them. Combinations of pewter and faïence or of pewter and glass are very agreeable.

Copper, brass and lead may be either hammered or cast. For the two former metals the design composed for hammered work should take account of the inconveniences which might arise from sharp projecting edges. It should, therefore, provide a properly curved moulding for the border. In the case of lead, the forms must not be too contorted, as the heaviness of the material would cause it to sag and lose its shape.

Zinc is usually stamped, and so can only be worked in thin sheets.

From the consideration of elements used directly in construction we pass naturally to manufactured ma-

terials. Plaster and stucco have, for centuries, been
well-known mediums. Adapting them to our use
we must bear in mind that imitation of stone is to be
avoided, false joints, heavy mouldings, stony rustications, etc., set aside. As a compensation, great
freedom in the use of projections, in fact, all the latitude
in which the modeler glories are at the disposition of
the designer. Stucco is usually painted or gilded,
and is especially appropriate for interiors.

The stucco work of Pompeii, and still more that of
the Arabs and Moors, offers most characteristic examples of cast designs. We may find a more modern
inspiration in later Italian and French decorations.
Although often executed with a ground work of wood
carving, these still present elements which are legiti-
mately translated in pure stucco. In Italian Renaissance we should study the Palazzo Spada and similar
palaces of Rome, the villas, the Palazzo Pitti, and the
ceilings of the ducal palace in Venice; in the French
Renaissance, the Gallerie de François I. at Fontaine-
bleau, the Louvre, Versailles, the Hotel Soubise and
other more restrained Louis XV. hotels; in our own
modern time the Paris Opera House, and the ceiling
of the Cour de Cassation in Paris. The last named
works, although, perhaps, overcharged with decoration,
are yet replete with ideas for the designer.

As may be seen by reviewing the foregoing examples, overcrowding of design is a besetting sin into
which the brilliant artist is likely to fall. A material
which offers no restrictions may easily be vulgarized
on account of lack of restraint in the fashioning.

Papier-mâché must be considered in somewhat the same category as stucco. It is of the greatest use, provided it makes no pretenses.

Imitation stone is always to be regretted. I do not mean that cement castings are to be eschewed, provided the design has broad elements appropriate to the material and the work does not pretend to be other than it is. It is the meretricious success sought through pretense and deceit that is damnable. Ruskin, whom we have so often quoted in the earlier chapters of this volume, has put forth too strong a plea for truth in architecture, for truth in art, to make possible any further addition to his glowing words.

It may here be allowable to speak of our American half-timber work in its use in connection with plaster and brick. Usually, because of expense, because of ill-seasoned wood, or to prevent the possibility of cracks that might extend through the wall, boards are used on top of the sheathing in imitation of the older construction. In a talk with one of our well-known American architects, this makeshift was championed on the ground that it is only a decoration, and intended to deceive no one. It seemed to me, however, that my friend was in reality trying to deceive himself.

We have already had occasion to speak of terracotta and of the uses to which it may be put. To sum up the subject: as long as pressed brick, tiles, and similar productions do not seek to imitate stone they may express the highest type of art. The designer should remember, however, that in moulding and baking, sharp definitions of plane may become softened.

Again, Greece, Rome, the East, Italy, France, with the northern countries, Flanders, the Netherlands, etc., offer us different and most useful suggestions. Very interesting effects may be obtained by the slight varying of the bond or design which bricks of unequal values accentuate in half-timber work. A study of similar work in Germany and England will repay the artist who intends to devote himself to domestic architecture. The soft, harmonious coloring of "Tapestry" brick offers a fertile field to the designer who is fond of color and wishes to use the material for its own sake.

The architect may also borrow successfully from the resources which enameled terra-cotta, faïence and porcelain so generously place before him. Be the subjects of decoration inspired from the wonderful creations of Lucca della Robbia and his followers, and set directly in stone, or be they Delft plaques used in combination with dark oak, the effect cannot fail to charm.

In general, the simpler the coloring, the better. Perhaps the safest sources of inspiration for purely decorative work (apart from the monochromes of Delft blues and browns) are those offered by Oriental designs, especially those of the Persians and Arabians. The artist must always keep in mind the distance from which his composition is to be seen. Porcelain medallions, and even plates, may be used with great decorative effect. Here the Chinese and Japanese are preëminent. Rookwood, Hartford, Wedgwood and similar faïences of our own modern times might be more used by architects.   Their mat tones are well adapted to dark wood.

Too great fineness is to be avoided in mosaic.   Inasmuch as the small blocks of stone must always cause irregularities in the drawing, the latter should be frankly conventional.   Perspective, especially for floorings, must be avoided.   The common arrangements (noted in Optical Effects) of tiles that seem to offer pointed blocks on which to walk are evidently irrational and inartistic.   Since the decorative characteristics are to predominate in mosaic, harmony and richness of color are the two great qualities to be sought.

The best examples may be found in Pompeian, Roman, Italian and in the Eastern work.   St. Mark's in Venice is noted for the warmth and almost barbaric glory of its mosaic decorations.   The Monreale mosaics are also well known.

There are some agreeable modern floor mosaics in the Paris Opera House.   The "Escalier Daru" of the Louvre has also lately been decorated with brilliant, perhaps not very successful, coloring.   In America we may be proud of the very attractive work in the lower floor of the Boston Public Library, where a quietness of design and charming harmony of color vie with each other in fixing our attention.   These mosaics are, however, modeled on the old Roman, or Italian work, which have not the daring and, of course, not the warmth of the more brilliant Byzantine compositions.

Cloisonné is a branch of art which has some things in common with mosaic.   Here again the design should be frankly conventional; indeed, this may be said of most enamels. China and Japan have furnished most beautiful specimens of cloisonné.

We have already spoken of the Boulle incrustation, so applicable to furniture designs. The inlaying of one metal in another, an earlier art much practiced in Spain and in the Orient, has hardly a place here. Such designs, while delicate, must remain either geometrical or conventional.

In making designs for transparent glass work, cut glass and even combinations of glass and metal, the artist should keep in mind that, not only will the surface in relief, but also the reverse of the other side be seen. Thus a plain portion may appear cut up by facets which the transparency of the material reveals.

A chapter of art especially interesting to the architect is that relating to stained glass. To go into an historical sketch of such a subject would be beyond the scope of this discussion. We need only quickly review the past in order to realize the changes which have taken place in the craft and in the designs for it.

Early windows were, of necessity, composed of small pieces of glass held together by leading. In all early work each color was represented by a separate piece of glass. Some modeling, draperies and the features of a face, etc., were painted in line in a dark brown pigment made of oxide of iron (iron rust) and fired in. Heavy painting was also used to stop out light between the lead contour and delicate silhouettes of the design. Colored windows had usually little white glass in them, and that attenuated by diaper pattern. The colored glass itself was what is known as pot-metal (glass with the color mixed in in the melting pot), and the effect was rich and brilliant. One of the chief qualities of old glass was its unevenness of color.

Early colored windows were usually medallion windows (the subjects were divided into small spaces or medallions with a border around the whole). The figures filled the space allotted to them, being detached either in light or dark on a simple ground of one color. This ground sometimes had a diaper pattern upon it. The drawing of the figures was naturally archaic; but this probably increased the decorative quality of the whole.

Grisaille windows, on the other hand, usually had little colored glass in their composition. The principal patterns were ornamental and drawn on white glass in the brown pigment before mentioned. Sometimes the ground was hatched in line to give it a darker tone.

Later on, as facility in manufacturing glass permitted the use of larger pieces, the size of the originally small subjects insensibly increased. Another aid to glaziers who wished to use large panes was the discovery of a manner of staining glass yellow. Flashed glass (one color coated with another) had always been known. With the new method many combinations could be obtained in a single pane. Given white and blue flashed together, the blue could be abraded in places and a portion of the white stained yellow. The blue could also be stained, adding green to the list.

But even this did not satisfy the Renaissance glass

workers, and they began to use enamel painting.
Here a color is mixed with powdered glass and the
mixture fired in.   Enamel never enters very well into
the pane, eventually peels, and, moreover, the result
does not give such rich color as does pot-metal glass.

In Renaissance glass a single picture, for it is pictorial effect that is aimed at, usually fills the whole
window ; and architecture is likely to play an important
rôle in the design.

Of late years, especially in English stained glass,
there has been a return to better conception of design,
marred by an overuse of paint.   Opalescent glass has
also been introduced in window work.

In our own day an American artist, John La Farge,
has had an immense influence on the art by his able
use of glass of varying thickness.   A heavy piece of
glass is eaten away by acids, to give high lights in the
thinner portions.   Thus pieces of glass of considerable size may be used, and variety of light and shade
obtained without the deadening of color and brilliancy which occurs when a foreign pigment is introduced.

Having come so far, let us examine the different
methods just described and try to appreciate their
qualities and faults.   The evident mission of stained
glass, not grisaille, is to present a *brilliantly*, as well
as harmoniously, colored decoration.   More than a
mural decoration or tapestry, more than a mosaic,
should glass profit by its chief characteristic, gem-like
radiance and warmth of color.   The qualities of glass
are distinctively decorative, and it follows that the

other phases of art, those which awaken an emotion or interest the mind, can only be secondary. Hence, the subject of a stained glass window should not be too predominant; should not show St. Denis standing in the flesh before us, his bloody head under his arm; nor should it even present the illustrious father of our country in fashion natural enough to convince us of his boyish integrity.

We find all of this fully expressed in old glass of the thirteenth, fourteenth and fifteenth centuries. The heavy leading, when not so evident as to force itself into prominence — a fault of the very old glass — gives a contrast which accentuates the rich colors of the design. There are examples of this at Chartres, Reims, the Sainte Chapelle, Notre Dame (in the famous north rose), Saint Etienne du Mont in Paris (glass in the cloister), the Duomo at Florence and of a slightly later date at Montmorency.[1]

A quality which the old glass possessed, a quality perhaps enforced by its limitations as well as by the taste of the artists, was almost uniform harmony. We have already seen that small bits of color, when placed together in a sort of mosaic, are much more likely to combine than large surfaces merely juxtaposed. Here the small size of the glass pieces and the necessity of considerable leading also enforced a conventional treatment, and diminished the temptation to realism, which a natural representation always presents.

[1] For a description of this glass see M. Lucien Magne's excellent Monograph; also Viollet le Duc.

The Renaissance period, with its large painted panes (the shadows were stippled), lost nearly all of these qualities. White glass, the usual ground, detracted through its high values in uncolored portions from the tarnished enamel coloring of the rest. Moreover, as we have already said, the decorative qualities gave place to incongruous, if not unskillful, pictorial effusions.

There is a distinct objection to the equal use, in the same design, of white and colored glass. In the first place, the effect of a colored window is diminished by curtailing the amount of color. But a still greater evil lies in the fact that white glass, high in value, blinds us to an appreciation of colored, while if the white is sufficiently deadened by paint, it becomes horny and disagreeable in effect. Of course, if much color is introduced into a grisaille window, it destroys the silveriness, its chief characteristic. Mr. Lewis F. Day in his excellent work entitled "Windows," speaking of the admixture of white and color at Reims and St. Denis, says:[1] "The amount of color introduced into grisaille was never at any time a fixed quantity; one has to allow something for the predilection of the artist; but here the amount of color makes itself so distinctly felt that the term grisaille no longer serves to express it. . . . It would have been difficult under any circumstances to produce a very satisfactory effect by so equally balancing white and color. The designer falls between two stools."

Approaching the English glass and opalescent work,

[1] Lewis F. Day, " Windows," London, B. T. Batsford & Co., 1897, pp. 119–120.

we cannot fail to find much pleasure in the quiet harmonies obtained by better designers, provided we close our mind's eye to the glorious masterpieces in old glass. For certain places, where a diffused and diminished lighting is a point in the program, opalescent glass may well claim a definite right of existence.

Last of all, considering the glass presented by Mr. La Farge and his school, we again see the true qualities of stained glass brought forward. The designer must, however, remember that here are no limitations to act as a safeguard against naturalism. He must be his own restrainer. If he indulges in too great thickness of glass he loses brilliancy as certainly as if he tarnished it; if he disdains leading he will fall into the faults presented by large quantities of the same color. He must keep his subject well within the realms of decorative art.

Let us recapitulate and add a few recommendations.

Colored glass is beautiful primarily because of its color; grisaille is so on account of the silvery light which it gives. In each case the treatment of the design should be decorative in character. Color and grisaille must not be evenly balanced in a window — the light ought to be either one thing or the other. The kind of window should be selected with regard to the place it is to decorate, and the character of the design would naturally be in keeping with that of the surrounding decoration. As to the treatment of the glass, the glazier need not be afraid of leads. They enhance the effect of the color and guard against too great realism. Moreover, a good design in the leading will always have a value of its own. If the design is in color the glass should be pot-metal; each piece glazed up separately, making what is called a mosaic window. Enamel is not brilliant and not lasting. Painted shadows and modeling ought to be as limited as possible. In La Farge and Tiffany, glass paint is only used for faces. The simple brown pigment is sometimes useful in diaper patterns to attenuate a too prominent color. Some drawing always seems necessary in the features of a face. It is better not to use tones of paint; even the stippled mat tones may be discarded and all shadows hatched. M. Mayeux, in his discussion of the subject, makes a plea for this. Grisaille and quarry patterns will, of course, be traced and hatched in paint.

Only experience and natural taste can dictate the combination and comparative values of colors and the amount of reduction or attenuation needful to make light bits of glass take their place at a distance. This, however, is not a text-book for glass workers, only a suggestion of the tendency which the art, as a part of decorative composition, should evince. Here it is enough to say that there must not be great contrasts in the values of glass in the same window. Colors which do not easily harmonize will usually be helped by the introduction of a white fillet or dark line between them; thus are blue and red prevented from fusing into purple.

A large piece of glass of one color is not agreeable. A ground may be leaded in several pieces; the easiest manner of leading is the best. Unequal glass always gives a better effect than does evenly toned.

A suggestion of M. Mayeux is that the dominant tones in a window should correspond to those of sky and climate; thus the greatest effect is obtained. The Dome des Invalides in Paris offers an interesting contrast of color in glass, which, if somewhat theatrical, is yet impressive. Here it is evident that, despite the climatic tonality, glass may still assert its own individuality. The general tone of the dome is given by slightly bluish glass diffusing a cold light, while on each side of the altar are brilliant orange windows, which seem to flood with sunshine the Holy of Holies.

When the sun is shining on one side of a building, some, perhaps all, of the windows are seen under unfavorable conditions; those catching the sunlight may be too brilliant and those in the shadow dimmed by excess of light in the interior. Therefore, in all countries not too far south, it is better to design for an overcast sky. Then one would only have to ask how much light the windows will usually receive. Perhaps one might use somewhat deeper tones in a south transept rose than in a north rose.

Before leaving the question of glass windows, there is a word to say about domestic work. Much more than has been done in pure ornamental glass design certainly remains to be done. It is possible that complicated, and, especially, deeply colored glass would be unsuited to a house, because light is needful. In most cases an attractive lead design is sufficient. If the window is not to be looked through, roundels, or bottle glass, may be used to advantage. Again, the introduction of a colored device or small cartouche may be acceptable. All must be in keeping with the rest of the interior.

Simple glass work may be useful for screens, or in the hundred other ways to be suggested by an ingenious imagination. We may also mention, *en passant*, the Arabian claustra set in white marble or in a white composition, translucent stone work and the use of alabaster. Such effects are very beautiful, but cannot be substituted for stained glass proper. Our own Tiffany Favril glass, so appropriate for lamp shades, vases and similar objects, might take a place in architectural design.

From the decorations appropriate to the holes in our walls we naturally pass to that of the walls themselves, *i.e.*, to mural painting.

Once more, our present duty is merely to unravel from the tangled skein of tendencies the manner best suited to the decoration of a building, through the painter's art. As in stained glass, a fresco (using the word in its popular sense) should first of all be essentially decorative. It should be pleasing to the eye. It differs from glass, however, in that it must make interesting a flat, opaque surface. The necessity for pure and brilliant coloring is, therefore, lessened, and in its place is substituted another requirement, which we may call "flatness." Since the coloring must play a secondary rôle, the subject may become more important; as a result, the composition, broad in scope and calculated for the distance from which it will be viewed, and the drawing should be carefully sought. Even here the subject matter ought not to contain harrowing suggestions, or should at least be so attenuated in interpretation that we feel ourselves before a printed page of description, not in the actual presence of a tragedy or crime.

It always happens that the room or hall where a fresco is placed has a definite destination, and naturally the subject matter of the painting will be somewhat predetermined; likewise the tonality, which must be selected to harmonize with the surrounding architecture.

En résumé, a wall painting must first, please, and second, interest. It should always remain flat and never induce the eye to believe real the objects portrayed. It must never make a hole in the wall. It is to harmonize with the architecture. Lastly, it should be appropriate to the especial place which it will occupy. To explain this we must speak of two distinct kinds of frescoes, viz.: those on a vertical and those on a horizontal surface or ceiling. The keynote of the requirements of each lies in one of our tenets: "Decoration should always be natural." In other words, while the compositions belonging to the first group should contain elements or figures which define a top and bottom in the design, those of the second should not usually tend toward any particular direction, and must always appear viewed from underneath. The Guido Reni Aurora in the Roman palace of the Rospigliosi, a composition evidently designed on a vertical surface, seems to fall upon the luckless observer. It is difficult to introduce architecture into a ceiling decoration without its seeming askew and ready to tumble. Where perspective is defined it is necessary arbitrarily to choose a point of view; in consequence, the composition and drawing are false from any other point.

The different methods of decorative painting are so well known that it may be out of place to describe them here. Real fresco must be done in water color while the plaster of the wall is fresh. Such work was sometimes retouched in tempora; color mixed with yolk of egg to give it sufficient adhesiveness. During Van Eyck's time oil painting was introduced into Italy, and mural painters began to work in this medium. Nowadays such work is often done on canvas in the studio, and later fastened in place. In order to avoid the brilliant surface presented by an oil painting, wax is sometimes mixed with the medium or the work may be done with turpentine or benzine on an absorbent canvas.

The best examples of mural painting are to be found in the old Pompeian work; the Byzantine, the early Italian of Giotto, Botticelli, etc. (the former is to be sought in Florence, but two exquisite frescoes of the latter are in the Musée du Louvre in Paris); the Renaissance as shown by Leonardo, Michael Angelo, and Raffaelle, later in the Venetian paintings of Paul Veronese and Tintoretto, and in the French work of Louis XVI. time, with that of Boucher, De la Roche, Flandrin and Baudry.

N

In spite of the beauty and lasting quality of the result, artists of the present day do not usually paint in real fresco, because of the difficulty and cumbersomeness of the process. Ingres tried to revive the art, and finally gave it up. Some of the northern painters, Carl Larsson, etc., have worked directly on the wet plaster.

After many abuses — painters skilled in representing nature are only too prone to forget their vows and attempt to make pictures instead of decorations — decorative painting had, at the end of the nineteenth century, reached a height as great as any attained in preceding years. This was due to Paul Puvis de Chavannes, who died with the century to which he lent such fame. His masterpieces combine all the qualities of a decoration, with wonderfully broad, with truly grand, conceptions of idea. Among the greatest of these works is the allegorical decoration in the amphitheater of the New Sorbonne; vieing with it, however, are the frescoes in the Escalier of the Musée de Picardie at Amiens. Other works are to be found in the Panthéon and Hotel de Ville in Paris, in Rouen, and in our own Boston Public Library.

Another modern French painter, Luc Olivier Merson, has given the world some very beautiful frescoes in those of the Palais de Justice in Paris. Interesting work of Besnard is to be found in the Ecole de Pharmacie and in the Salle de Mariage of the Mairie of the Ier Arrondissement in the same city.

Of the English painters of modern times, Rossetti and Burne Jones possess decorative qualities; but the tendencies of such schools seem almost too affected for paintings which are to be permanently in place. In America E. H. Blashfield's numerous beautiful decorations hold our attention.

The work of John Sargent in the Boston Public Library is of great interest, as is also some of that in the Congressional Library in Washington. Confusion, however, should be avoided in a decoration, and this is unfortunately the fault of many modern painters.

It is impossible to enumerate all the modern sources of inspiration for the student. Happily, true inspiration comes from within, not from without.

There are branches of decorative drawing and painting other than those appertaining to mural decoration, branches which must also be of greatest interest to the architect. The field, which includes pen and ink work, illustrating, designing of book covers, posters, etc., lies halfway between the realm of the painter and that of his brother artist. Some of our younger architects have already made a name in these directions, while the more legitimate proprietors of the brush have come to meet them.

One of the best known portrayers of architectural subjects is Joseph Pennell, but the manners of the different men vary to such an extent that it would be as difficult to make a comparison as it would be wrong to imitate any one of them. Let the student keep in mind that direct study and practice are alone of use, that conscientiousness is better than chic, that indication always means good drawing. Let him take his time, and yet work as simply as possible, never drawing more than he sees.[1]

As to posters, above all, they must "carry." They should be simple bits of decoration attracting the attention and legible from a distance. Naturally, another essential is that they be characteristic of the subject they announce. The list of names noted for poster work is too long and too changeable to give here; Chéret, Grasset, Steinlen and their fellows were known a few years ago and are now being forgotten. Evidently, such fame is not durable.

Another group in decorative design is that filled by stamped leather, burnt leather and wall paper. Here again the decorative qualities must be preëminent. It is to be regretted that leather is not more extensively used in interior decoration. The Spanish and French work, and especially the Flemish stamped or gilded leather designs of the sixteenth century should be a great inspiration.

In wall paper designing M. Mayeux[2] gives some excellent suggestions. Making his plea for conventional treatment, he advises against the introduction of animals, excepting only heraldic figures. He also advises against the portrayal of a too direct or precise lighting; the shadows are sure to be in contradiction with the real lighting of some part of the room where the paper is hung. Another fault he notes is the tendency of some designers to introduce details of

---

[1] An interesting review of the art of the pen is "Pen Drawing and Pen Draughtsman," by Joseph Pennell. London, Macmillan.

[2] La Composition Décorative, p. 281.

small scale. All suggestions of depth in the design should be avoided. Last of all, he deplores the attempts, cherished by manufacturers, to make wall papers resemble an hundred and one other substances— leather, canvas, velvet, etc. The subject of wall paper leads us to a review of the question of tapestries, an art of which the former is in a measure the descendant.

In trying to define the requisites of tapestry design, I shall quote from M. Eugène Müntz's review of the question in "La Tapisserie." Since tapestries are intended for decorations of richly furnished rooms, grace the reunions of a brilliant society, or, even more, are often used only to lend distinction to public festivals, the character of the design, subject, composition and coloring should be brilliant and sumptuous.

On page 11 of La Tapisserie [1] he says : "Nous nous serions bien mal exprimé s'il ne résultait jusqu'à l'évidence, des considérations qui précèdent, que la tapisserie est un art essentiellement somptuaire, inséparable de l'idée de magnificence, et destiné à charmer, à séduire, à éblouir bien plus qu'à instruir ou émouvoir. L'expression de la souffrance ou de l'abnégation, les hautes conceptions philosophiques, l'austérité, ne sont point de mise ici. Disposant des factures les plus parfaits de l'art textile, de tous les raffinements de la teinture, la soie, les fils d'argent et d'or, le pourpre, l'écarlate, on ne s'opiniâtrera pas à rechercher les colorations ternes à traduire les idées lugubres."

[1] Eugène Müntz, "La Tapisserie," Paris, Librairies Imprimeries Réunies.

He goes on to say that in choice of subject those which are too intimate, which contain too few personages, should be set aside. As to the arrangement of the composition, he favors a distribution of the interest over the whole design and decries too fine a finish. This he sustains because of the characteristics which the design should possess and also because the tapestry itself, once hung, must necessarily be more or less displaced and distorted: [1] "Il faut, d'une part, ne pas reculer devant l'abondance des détails, multiplier les figures de mainère à produire un groupement très nourri; de l'autre donner à l'action cette régularité, cette pondération, cette tenue sans lesquelles il n'y a point d'art décoratif." He adds that the arrangement lauded by Charles Blanc in the Grammaire des Arts Décoratifs, placing the point of sight very high in the composition, in order that the whole may be filled with figures, may be useful, but not absolutely necessary. He recommends the arrangement in the form of a frieze, and goes on to speak of the treatment of the distance in a tapestry: "Veut-on donner plus de profondeur a la composition, j'insisterai sur la nécessité de soutenir les figures du premier plan par un fond très nourri, notamment par des vues d'architecture." Müntz also countenances the introduction of subjects foreign to the main composition, provided they be decorative.

M. Mayeux considers the high point of sight unnecessary. He condemns the introduction of heavy shadows which, of necessity, make dark and undecora-

[1] "La Tapisserie," p. 10.

tive blots. Speaking of the border, Mayeux remarks [1]
that it may be treated as though in front of, in the
same plane with, or (as a mat) behind the subject.
In the first and third cases the scale of the border is
usually different from that of the subject. Farther
on he remarks that although the general coloring of
the border and subject may be different, they should
not only harmonize, but some notes of the border colors
should be found in the main composition.

Müntz deplores the manner in which certain artists
of the later Renaissance have tried to imitate gold
frames in the design of the border. He praises [2] the
borders which Raffaelle composed for the celebrated
suite of the Acts of the Apostles: "C'est tout un
monde que ces bordures, d'ont les motifs se déroulent
tantôt avec le calme majesté d'un bas-relief antique
et tantôt jaillissent, se pressent, se multiplient comme
les étincelles d'un feu d'artifice. Le maître y a pro-
digué les figures les plus nobles, les Parques, les Heures,
les Saisons, Hercule supportant le globe terrestre, et
des ornements d'une grace achevée: termes, satyres,
grotesques, lion reposant sous une branche de laurier,
vases de fleurs d'un galbe admirable, banderoles,
écussons, les plus beaux produits de la nature et les
plus belles inventions de l'art."

As a general recommendation, the more the tones
of a tapestry are simplified the better. If the initia-
tive were still left to the weaver, that he, like his predecessors, might use his judgment and interpret in-

[1] "La Composition Décorative," p. 286.
[2] "La Tapisserie," p. 189.

stead of copy the models, undoubtedly the tendency
to make historical pictures of tapestries would be
lessened. The almost infinite number of colors and
tones now at the disposition of the tapestry weaver
is a subject for commiseration rather than congratu-
lation.

Designing for a carpet, no perspective should be
indulged in, nor should shadows which suggest relief
be depicted. The subject, distinctly conventional,
ought, as with mosaic, never to contain elements on
which one would hesitate to walk. The same may be
remarked of designs for furniture, seats of chairs, etc.

During the fourteenth century the best tapestries
came from the looms of northern France and Flanders,
especially from those of Paris and Arras. During the
fifteenth century Arras eclipsed Paris, but finally, toward the end of the century, in 1479, the expulsion of
her inhabitants, by Louis XI., closed the scene of her
glories.

The palm for the manufacture of tapestries was
held by Brussels during the end of the fifteenth century and the greater part of the sixteenth century,
and in the latter period, we also see Italy coming to
the fore. Moreover, the Italian artists of the Renaissance exercised a dominating influence on tapestry
design, and were called upon to furnish cartoons even
outside of their own country.

In the early part of the seventeenth century Henry
IV. of France began to encourage the manufacture
of tapestry at Paris, and founded several ateliers.
In 1662 Louis XIV. founded the justly famed Manu-

facture des Gobelins, a wise step which he followed
up in 1667 by founding those of Beauvais. Le Brun
was chosen as director of the Gobelins, and to him are
due not only some of the best cartoons which have
been painted as tapestry models, but as well the excellent policy which lent such just fame to his charge.

Under Louis XV., Oudry and Boucher exercised a
pernicious influence in curtailing the liberty of interpretation accorded to the weavers. Boucher's designs, however, are charming, and, in spite of the want
of elevation in his choice of subject, truly decorative.

In 1625 a new center had been established for the
manufacture of tapestries. James II. of England
installed the looms at Mortlake, and these, under the
judicious management of Sir Francis Crane, ranked
for half a century as leaders in the art.

The decadence, begun in the eighteenth century,
continued on into the nineteenth. Of late years so
much has been said on this subject and such sincere
efforts are being made to restore to the ancient art
some of its earlier integrity, that the optimistic already foresee a new Renaissance.

In seeking sources of inspiration for the study of
carpet design we must turn to the East once more.
Arabia, Persia, Asia Minor, etc., are the countries
whose carpets have hitherto outrivaled, and still
surpass, all of which the West can boast.

PART V

CHAPTER I

Composition in Plan

To read rules for the construction of a plan will never make the aspirant an architect. The thousand and one details which the designer must notice; the characteristics, whether conventional or logical, which he must feel; above all, the ability to reason out the necessities of a plan, to arrange them in his mind, and finally transcribe them on paper, these three different requisites for successful composition can only be acquired by years of practice. Naturally, an office training will help in the first, and a wide horizon in every-day life in the second, while a thorough study of pure mathematics, geometry, etc., will prepare the mind for the third. But only attempts at composing (the weeding out of a program and final fulfillment of its clauses, and above all, of its title), seconded by sound criticism, can finally form the architect and distinguish him from the decorator.

And so, at first, it seems almost useless to write lengthily on the subject. However, remembering how much I myself wished for some definite and tabulated recommendations, I feel it wise to make a few suggestions, which, if not all sufficient, may at least be of use to another.

First, the rules which apply to composition in plan are, in essence, those which apply to other kinds of composition. We must have Truth, Sincerity, Honesty and Character, and in the technical considerations, a climax, with a proper leading up of minor parts that contrast in their arrangement. This may all sound pictorial, but only the casual reader will fail to see truth in the assertion.

Truth and honesty in a plan mean that the design expresses what it pretends to be; inversely, shall correspond to the program. Many able architects are prone to disregard this, and thereby bring the greatest discredit on the profession. A business man, or committee of men, having studied the question of need and knowing how much money they can invest, go to an eminent architect and ask for a definite practical result. The architect accepts the charge; but, full of what he considers artistic ideas, fails to pay proper attention to the future uses of the building; and later on, when the owners discover that they have spent good money, and are yet deprived of a good investment, they dub their architect (very justly), if not a thief, at least a bungler. Some of the most attractive looking buildings in America show practical and, from the point of view of plan, most regrettable faults.

Of course, it sometimes happens that an ignorant or dishonest committee, rather than the architect, may be to blame. Into such questions we cannot go.

Unluckily, no profession, and architecture must, sad to say, be a profession as well as an art, is free from bad practices. The truly conscientious man, when he has only the choice of discreditable work or no work, would decide for no work, and thus be likely to gain in the end. Although minus a certain sum in commissions, his reputation would remain intact. Let him never imagine, however, that to insist on an impractical solution is a virtue. It is here that the distinction comes in. The architect should be thankful to an owner who saves him from being unpractical, despite the irksomeness of having to commence anew.

As in our first inquiry, we find that Character is merely Honesty in another guise. We may define it as the quality which announces the destination and use of a plan.

Plans may, generally speaking, be divided into two kinds, *i.e.*, the one which has an exterior silhouette, and that enclosed between given lines (party walls, etc.). Compositions for the country usually come under the former head and those for a city, where every bit of ground must be utilized, under the second. This distinction in shape is most important in deciding the category in which a plan must be placed; and it is as much a fault to bring down to four straight lines one whose silhouette should be an attractive element as it would be to waste space in a city, and set the building back from the street.

Another element which greatly influences the general aspect of a plan is the character of the ground — whether it is inclined or not, etc. When the ground is inclined the different buildings of the composition should all be designed with their longest axis or greatest dimensions perpendicular to the line of greatest inclination of the ground. This is another essential. Moreover, it usually happens that when ground is inclined there is a view of which to take advantage. In such a case the plan must "open out" at the bottom, presenting the general form of an inverted V. Fig. 68 shows different forms of this, *a* being a mistaken closing in at the bottom, while *b* only becomes good when the inclination is very steep. Considering individual buildings, the greatest length should be toward the view.

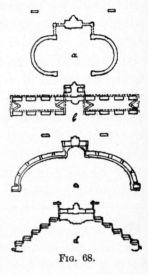

FIG. 68.

We see thus that ground formation is a second factor in determining the shape of a plan. The artist takes advantage of what nature sets before him; only the unskillful try to change nature by impossible earthworks. In landscape gardening (an art that comes directly within the dominion of the planner), realization of this is all important.

Before definitely leaving the present subject, it may be well to mention some exceptions permissible when placing buildings on an inclined ground. It is allowable to build light passageways, inclined or with frequent flights of steps, parallel to the line of greatest inclination, and at times, although rarely, it is better to place a group of short buildings perpendicular to the line of inclination, rather than each building of the group. A glance at Fig. 69 will explain this. M. Deglane one day remarked, during a criticism, "The architect can never have perfection. He must always choose the lesser of two evils."

FIG. 69.

Another most important factor giving character to a plan is the use and its resultant interior arrangement and indication. Naturally, there are certain peculiarities which define differences between plans of marked characteristics. A large department store or an office building would be utterly unlike an opera house with its circular auditorium. But we must go farther than such mere outposts and remember that there are elements of dissimilarity between the opera house and the concert hall, nicer distinctions none the less indispensable. The opera house needs in its decoration a more important treatment, brilliant, because a place of amusement, but refined and with a certain restrained or even classical feeling. The concert hall (the more popular class) might still have a semicircular auditorium, but the decoration should be lighter and gayer. As a result, the "points" (piers) would not present the same surface, would not translate simple wall space which must act as a "repoussoir." If architects but keep in mind the decoration and later construction of their buildings, they will not fail in indication in plan.

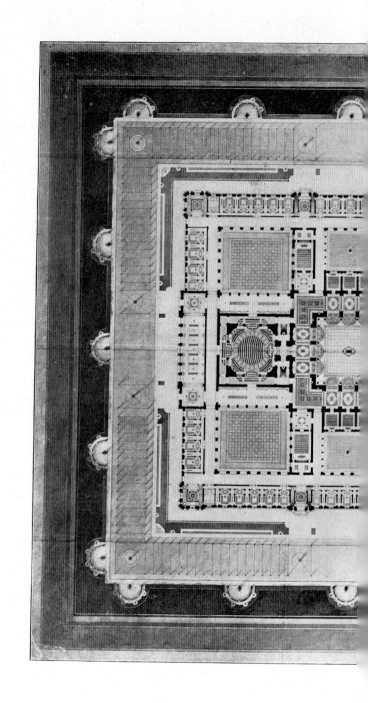

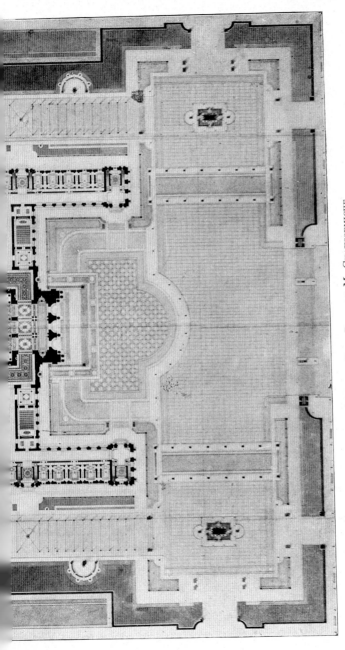

Fig. 70. — Grand Prix Plan of M. Chaussemiche.

We may well add a few general directions to guide the beginner in interpreting broad classes of buildings. Where the public is to come, make ample all the approaches, entrances, exits and general effects. Where there are to be reception rooms, from the French point of view, there should always be a court of honor, "Celui qui dit 'Hotel' dit 'Cour d'Honneur.'" This, perhaps, is less true in America. The charming plans of the Louis XV. "hotels," as shown in existing examples, and also in the designs of Blondel, Briseux and other artists of the time, had their courts of honor on the side toward the street, and (a most sensible arrangement, which we moderns might well copy) delightfully arranged gardens behind, overlooked by all the reception and living rooms. When a program implies a conglomeration of persons who must remain within the limits of the buildings (such as a barracks or a school), the chief element of the plan should be a large court or open space. It is not an exaggeration to say that the whole should seem rather a plan of a quadrangle, with buildings on the outskirts. Last, where a comparison of work and study-rooms occurs (as in a manual training school), the former should occupy very many times the space given up to the latter.

We have said that the technical laws for arranging a plan are those which apply to all compositions. Turning back to our summary of laws (page 41), we remember that there must be a climax or focal point placed in the most important position; that all other elements must lead up to the climax and contrast in their inter-relations; and that the whole must have harmony. In planning, then, our most important element, perhaps a public reception hall in the White House, the high altar in a church, the auditorium and stage in a theater should still be given the most important position.

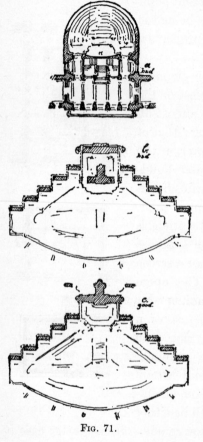

FIG. 71.

And what is this most important position? In a symmetrical plan it will naturally be on the principal axis. But where on that axis? Generally speaking, at the back or head of the plan, provided we have a simple composition before us, not requiring an important posterior entrance. The Grand Prix plan of M. Chaussemiche (Fig. 70) is such a solution. Here, then, is the definite rule, viz.: in the usual plan, having no important posterior entrance, the climax should be at the back, and approach along the axis should be kept entirely open. Fig. 71 shows two violations of this, which yet at first sight might seem feasible. The desire to reach an upper floor, in attractive fashion, leads to the blocking of the approach to the main feature. In *b*, designed for inclined ground, the important point itself blocks the axis by being too far forward; *c* is the proper arrangement.

The average student is strongly tempted to place a staircase on the axis; yet it is fatal in almost all cases except the following : that of the opera house or theater, of the State Capitol, and similar buildings, and of the library whose reading room is on an upper floor. The reason for these exceptions is evident enough, for the staircase becomes an access to, not a screen before, the climax. The opera house of Paris is an eminent example of the successful use of a monumental staircase, placed on axis as an approach to the important feature of the composition.

When a staircase is on an important axis, it may well be either a straight or a triple motive one. In the latter case it should begin to rise in the middle, then turn to right and left, or even return again (Fig. 72, *a* and *b*). Other uses of the triple motive staircase are absurd; yet one often finds it in the designs of beginners, tucked away on

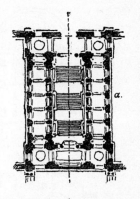
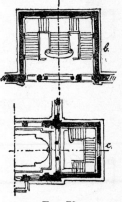

Fig. 72.

o

one side, where, considering only the waste of space entailed, it would be far more sensible to use a simple "escalier à la Française," turning always in the same direction (c, Fig. 72). When such a staircase occurs on one side of a small plan it is not at all necessary to balance it with a useless repetition on the other, provided it is possible to see the stairs from the entrance. The last condition is important, because otherwise the public might make a start in a false direction.

A last general recommendation is that the lowest step of a monumental staircase should be set back from the entrance to the stair hall or cage. This allows of a pause on the level, permitting the public to appreciate the decoration, before the ascent is begun.

In exterior compositions, where an avenue (of approach to a city, perhaps, or in an analogous case) occupies the axis, it is especially important to keep the entrance at the bottom of the plan entirely free from either buildings or decorative motives. Again, and it cannot be too often repeated, the bottom of a plan should be open.

In many large plans it happens that two main entrances (from front and rear) must be provided. In a large school, for instance, where exposition rooms, or an auditorium, are designed with entrance for the public, it may well occur that the students' entrance is better placed on the opposite side. The plan then becomes an X in form, each side leading up to the central point. M. Henri Deglane's Grand Prix (Fig. 73) is a noted solution of this kind. See also those of M. Bigot and M. Tournaire (Figs. 88 and 89). The

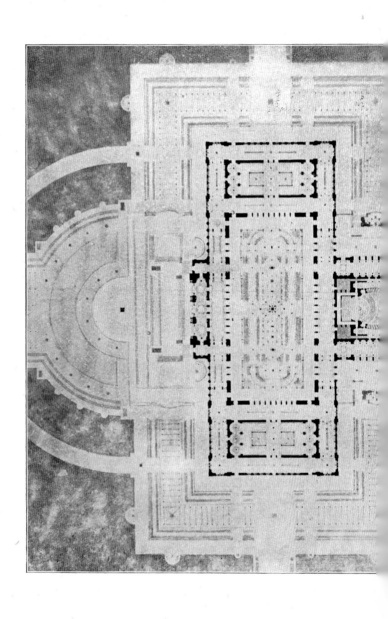

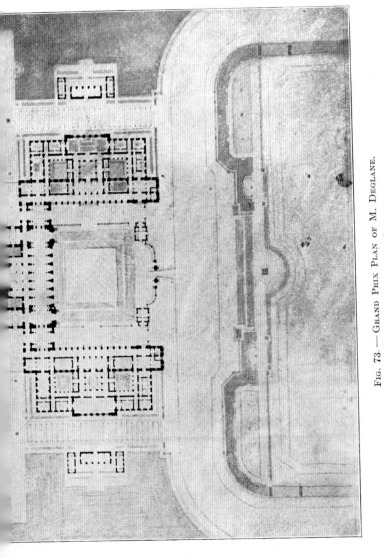

Fig. 73. — Grand Prix Plan of M. Deglane.

former shows an approach from the sea on one side
and from the town on the other. The whole plan,
designed for a naval academy, has much character.

We must also speak of plans having two main
vertical axes. In such an instance, the two points
of interest will be joined by a main horizontal axis
uniting the composition (Fig. 74). As already said
in our general classification (page 81), this is an unusual
case, only to be used by excep-
tion, where an entrance exists
on the right and an exit on the
left. An unsymmetrical composition naturally throws the
principal motive out of the
middle of the composition. It
should be balanced as we have
described on page 46. M.
Duquesne's Grand Prix design

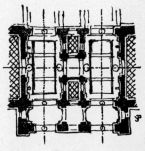

FIG. 74.

(Fig. 75) is an example of an unsymmetrical arrangement selected on account of the ground formation.

Having discussed the general character of plans,
their aspect and main forms of composition, we are
ready to study the lesser elements and decide how
they may best unite with each other and the principal
motive. This is really "Le Groupement des Services," forming and arranging groups of different details.

The principal motive set aside, we select the next
important elements of the program, remembering that
like uses define the general placing. Indeed, the first
preoccupation of the designer is to sort out and group

different species of rooms (public, private, scholastic, the dining rooms, kitchen, and accessories, sleeping rooms and dormitories, etc.), rather than to study the definite arrangement of each room. All of the lesser groups must lead from the main ones in the most practical and convenient order. Thus, in M. Chaussemiche's plan (Fig. 70), a large court, or central space, makes a point from which one can find the different lecture halls and class rooms, and so unifies a special major group. Nevertheless, the axis is kept open, and the whole leads to the main feature of the plan, the large auditorium.

A number of similar rooms should form a suite, and the more monotonous such a suite the better. We see this also in M. Chaussemiche's plan, where the small class rooms or laboratories make a frame about the public central group. The disposition is especially good, giving excellent light, retirement and separate access to rooms where study is the motive. The beginner must remember that a series of quite similar rooms is never to be divided into two balancing groups. As in the plan just cited, those on the right must follow around to those on the left. A disregard of this suggests to the facetious observer that a Quaker meeting is to take place, the men being carefully kept on one side and the women on the other.

Last, but not least (indeed, in designing some plans, it is here that we should begin our construction, the skeleton of our figure), comes the question of "circulation." (It seems best to adopt the French term, as "halls" or "passages" do not imply all that is meant.)

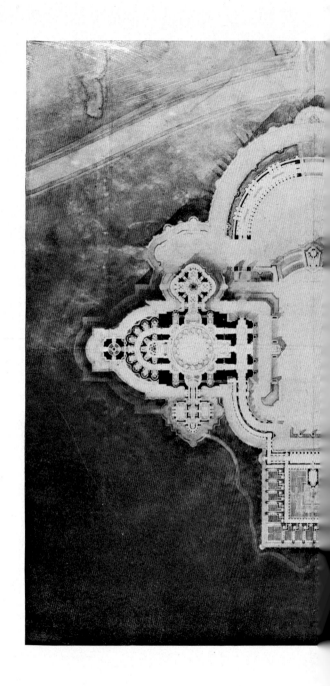

FIG. 75. — GRAND PRIX PLAN OF M. DUQUESNE.

In a plan where the public is to enter, or in one where a crowd may have to pass at a given moment, do not be afraid of ample corridors. Such circulations should pass from group to group without interruption, yet not cut off part of a group. All of the plans here cited as examples are excellent in this respect, for well arranged circulations are an essential of good planning; but those of MM. Chaussemiche, Deglane and Tournaire (Figs. 70, 73, and 89) will repay especial study.

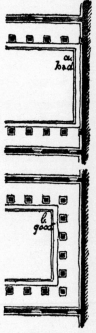

The recommendation not to break any circulation extends even to the introduction of passages that have only an indirect use. If (Fig. 76) a suite of rooms runs up to a party wall, the corridor which connects them should continue around the fourth unused side of the court. *a* of Fig. 76 shows a broken circulation, *b* an unbroken one.

A circulation can be faultily broken by one of another class, *i.e.*, the passage reserved for the public might be

FIG. 76.

severed by a crossing of carriages or by a service hall (from kitchen to dining room).

Circulations and passages are among the most important factors in tying together different parts of a plan. The carrying, or tying through of walls, a requirement of sensible planning, indeed, of good construction, is another means. Also, most important is the preservation of the axes of avenues, openings, rooms, or other elements to be connected. If all of these methods fail, we may ask ourselves whether the building, or portion of building, is not out of place, whether it is not merely an afterthought. Among such mistaken adjuncts, elements that can never be successfully tied into a composition, is the small porter's lodge, lean-to at the entrance of a building. These, beginners are

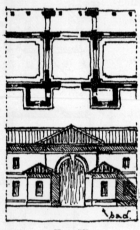

likely to add, because a clause of the program requires some provision for the service. Fig. 77 shows such faulty additions.

In general, an entrance motive should be slightly broken out in advance of the main wall of the façade, when it would in consequence rise higher in its decoration. The limit is to place it in the same plane with the rest of the façade. It should never be behind the plane (*a*, *b* and *c* of Fig.

FIG. 77.

78). This bringing forward of the entrance motive should not be great, however, as otherwise, in perspective, the effect of the elevation is diminished (*d*, Fig. 78). In saying that the entrance motive should not be sunk in the wall, no reference to the court of honor is intended. This latter is of excellent effect in perspective. Students need only keep in mind that the central space must be considerably wider than the wings, and at most not set back more than once and a half its width (Fig. 78, *e* and *f*).

"Air in a plan" is the quality presented when there is no apparent crowding of the elements. All plans should have as much "air" as possible; but those situated in the country or on unenclosed ground must

be especially open. This is obtained by massing the courts and open spaces, keeping the arrangement simple. All rooms and passages (except vaults, etc.) should have direct opening on large courts or on the street. We are too liable, in America, to content ourselves with light shafts, sky-lights, or other halfway contrivances, which proper study on the part of the architect might obviate without loss of space.

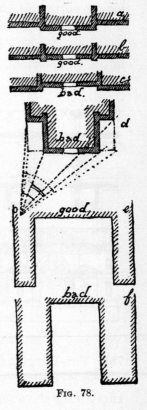

FIG. 78.

Extra doubling of passages and rows of rooms should be avoided. No wing ought to have more than one doubling when the central space is long or cannot be well lighted from the end. Thus Figs. 79, *a* and *b*, allow of direct lighting of the passage *P*, but *c* should not be used. Except in special cases the auditorium or lecture hall closed in by passages on both sides is to be avoided. Never add an extra passage merely for symmetry. Rather than such a useless and objectionable balancing, a new scheme should be adopted.

In order to show, in practical manner, the method of analyzing, or rather of synthesizing, a plan, we shall take a program and explain the making of the sketch for it. The subject following is that of a problem

studied by the students under me at Cornell, and I can thus supply the different schemes used at the time by various men, and add a word or two of criticism.

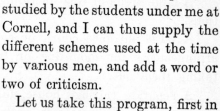

Let us take this program, first in the confused form in which one might find such a list of requirements, and then sort it out. I remember an eminent French architect once saying that a poor program was like "a basket containing flowers

and fruit, cabbages, potatoes and roses, all thrown together pellmell." The designer has to turn the whole in a heap and pick out the different varieties, arranging those of a kind together, before he can proceed with the cooking of his dinner or the setting and decorating of his table.

The subject of our program is, "A Riding Club."

FIG. 79.

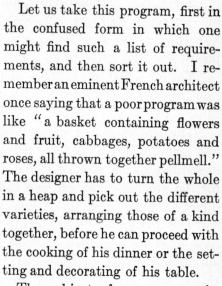

"A number of wealthy gentlemen having formed a riding club, wish to erect a building with the necessary equipment. Provision should be made for instruction and exhibition in horsemanship and for stabling members' riding horses.

"The general scheme shall consist of:

"Stables for 160 horses.

"A large arena or ring for riding lessons and exhibitions.

"A large entrance court, or court of honor, with arrangements for mounting or trying horses before taking them out.

"A separate carriage house, for a limited number of carriages; also quarters with dining room and kitchen, for the attendants, while an office may be placed with the latter group if it be near the entrance.

"The lot is 300 feet square. The principal entrance shall be on a broad avenue with small streets on the other three sides of the lot.

"The stables shall connect directly with the court and arena. They shall have necessary adjuncts, such as harness rooms, storage rooms, hay lofts and rooms for the grooms. The carriage house shall also be in direct communication with the court.

"The arena may be rectangular in form and should have 16,000 square feet of floor area. A gallery for spectators should be provided; also, near the entrance two groups, each of twenty dressing rooms (for men and women), with adequate bathing facilities. A central reception room shall be added, as well as a committee room and offices. The arena shall have an exit for horses to the court.

"The stables may be divided into two groups, one for the horses belonging to the club proper and the other for those belonging to the members. Service courts are necessary to the stables."

The scales of the drawings required will not be of interest to us at present.

In order to correct or sort out the program, the designer must necessarily have some idea of what are the requirements of a riding club. He must, however, be careful to permeate himself with the spirit of the program; to find out what the man who wrote it really meant; to add nothing to, or take nothing from the first writing, no matter in what changes of order of expression he may see fit to indulge. The most important items should come first, and so, going on down the scale, he would arrive at something like the following:

"A RIDING CLUB"

"A number of wealthy gentlemen having formed a riding club, wish to erect a building, with the necessary equipment. Provision should be made for instruction and exhibition in horsemanship and for stabling members' horses.

"The general scheme shall consist of:

"1. A large entrance court, or court of honor, with arrangements for mounting or trying horses before taking them out.

"2. A large arena or ring for riding lessons and exhibitions, with exit for horses to the court. The arena may be rectangular in form, and should have about 16,000 square feet of floor area. A gallery for spectators should be provided; also, near the entrance two groups, each of twenty dressing rooms (for men and women), with adequate bathing facilities. A central reception room shall be added, as well as a committee room and offices.

" 3. Stables (for 160 horses), opening into both court and arena, with necessary adjuncts, such as harness rooms, storage rooms, hay lofts and rooms for the grooms.

" The stables may be divided into two groups, one for the horses belonging to the club proper and the other for those belonging to the members. Service courts are necessary to the stables.

" 4 and 5. A separate carriage house in direct communication with the court shall be provided for a limited number of carriages; also, quarters with dining room and kitchen for the attendants, while an office may be placed with the latter group if it be near the entrance.

" The lot is 300 feet square.

" The principal entrance shall be on a broad avenue, with small streets on the other three sides of the lot."

Having put our program in order (an unnecessary preliminary when it has been properly written), the next duty of the architect is to impress himself deeply with the title. From this title he should draw his realization of the character of the design.

"A Riding Club." It is then primarily for the purpose of riding, and must show that in all its expressions and appurtenances. But more than this, it is also a club, not a public, but a private enterprise, and the private enterprise of cultured, of wealthy persons. Here is a second set of characteristics which must show in the design. Nothing must be stinted, and all refined. No show for advertisement, no vulgarity, and yet perfect, even luxurious, appointments.

Then comes a reading of the descriptive paragraph, where these indications of character are strengthened. In this paragraph the practical aims of the club are also set forth: instruction, exhibitions of the result, and arrangements for future exercise. The plan must further these three needs. For the first, the club members must have every convenience; for the second, not only the members, but a public of visitors must be received; for the third, the members must find a practical disposition of the service, allowing prompt attention. We have mentioned no cost, but when such a clause appears it should be rigorously adhered to, and although it ought not to influence the character, it should decidedly influence the design in choice of kind of construction, etc.

Let us now take up the items of the program: here it may be well to say that a program should be read over several times, carefully thought out, and all possible dispositions considered, before pencil is put to paper. First of all comes a court of honor. It must be first (in the case of a symmetrical composition, on the axis), because of its qualities, expressed in the program by the words court *of honor* or *entrance* court. Then, there is the arena, and that is evidently the principal point of the program, the climax. So it will go at the back, or at least in the important part of the plan; this too, on the axis, if a symmetrical composition is used. The stables can be separated into two groups so they would easily balance; and we have two smaller groups, 4 and 5, which can also balance. Therefore, there is no reason for adopting an unsymmetrical composition; and we may discard that from the list of possibilities.

Let us return to our court. The clauses which insist on the arena, stables and carriage house opening directly from the court, imply that in a measure it is to be a center of radiation. It must be conveniently arranged for the mounting and trying of horses. It must also be so disposed, with regard to the arena, that the members, and especially visitors, can reach the arena without experiencing discomfort or danger proceeding from the same mounting and trying. Therefore, the approach along the axis to the arena must be clear and more or less protected, while the exits for the horses to the court and streets, from the arena and stables, ought not to interfere with the central walk. Inasmuch as visitors may arrive in carriages, they should be able to drive up to the arena without interfering with the other uses of the court.

The arena may well be long rather than square, giving in the hippodrome form even a better sweep than that of the circular ring. Either shape, however, is permissible. The reception and committee rooms, with the gallery staircase, should be centrally and conspicuously placed at the entrance to the arena building, that the public shall need no directions. Dressing and bath rooms are more private; being in two separate groups they may be relegated to right and left. The offices, naturally, should be in full view at the entrance.

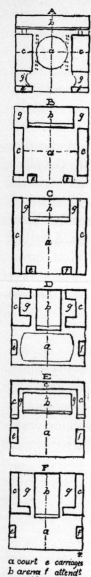

a court   e carriages
b arena   f attend't
cc stables gg service

FIG. 80.

The stables must fulfill a twofold requirement : of accessibility to the arena and to the court. The especial requisites of stables will be studied in the sixth part of this volume. As to the carriage house and attendants' building — although easy to reach, they should not interfere with the effect of the court.

We may now begin to formulate definite schemes for our plans, deciding roughly what relative sizes the different buildings must eventually have. The arrangement that immediately occurs to us is *A* of Fig. 80. Two exits from the arena to the court would open into a circular drive, with space on the outer sides, which would allow room for the mounting of horses. The court should be made as large as possible. *B* (Fig. 80) might be our second idea ; *C, D, E* and *F*, others. In *A* the dressing and bath rooms, etc., would make a doubling in front of the arena, difficult of treatment in façade. In *D* and *F* the axis of the stables and stable courts would probably correspond to that of the ring proper, the dressing rooms, etc., projecting in front. This has the inconvenience of diminishing the court in width just where it should be broadest. In *E* the composition is an attractive one, but the service courts would be narrow, and yet take up much space on account of their length. This diminishes the court of honor.

Once having projected all the schemes we can think of, we should leave our work for a short time, and then, returning to it fresh, weigh carefully the merits and demerits of each plan, finally selecting the best. This we should draw to scale, using appropriate indication to assure ourselves that no flaws exist. With the plans we shall have imagined our elevations and sections. These we also draw out; and if serious difficulties occur, it might be necessary to go back to a discarded plan. It often happens that the final scheme selected is that of our first idea; so here, perhaps, the most direct arrangement is A. Its stables, however, will always mask the façade of the arena, whereas B, C, D, E and F leave the latter quite clear.

Further study of the sketch means a careful redrawing of the whole, or at least of parts, on successive pieces of tracing paper — five, ten, twenty times, if need be. We begin with masses and end by going into the smallest details; first at a small scale, then at double. Finally come the exhibition or working drawings — but we are going beyond our province.

CHAPTER II

INDICATION

In indication of plan, the different elements may be divided into two main groups: piers ("points") and walls, or "poché" and "mosaic."

An axiom in the arrangement of "points" is that breaks which occur in one must be found of equal depth in another opposite. Thus the silhouette a, b, c, d of B (Fig. 81) should correspond to the silhouette a', b', c', d'. The axis of the opening must be that of all minor breaks. There are exceptions to this, of course. If the designer realizes in imagination the construction and decoration to be expressed, he will know when the breaks on one side would interpret a flat wall space above the springing of the arches, and so correspond to a flat surface on the opposite side of the opening or passage, C (Fig. 81).

The power of seeing a completed figure in the mind's eye is acquired by a thorough training in descriptive geometry. It is more or less natural to some, but through practice any one can finally attain facility, provided he never draws a silhouette in plan without knowing what it means.

And now we must find out exactly what is meant by "axes" in a plan. The broad term is used to designate great constructive lines of symmetry on which the whole is built, the skeleton of the plan. But in a lesser way, what is an axis, and what are the limitations which may be applied to its use?

I remember an "ancien" of the *Ecole* once remarking epigrammatically that an axis implied an opening, that the term "axis of a point" meant nothing. And this is true, because the need of an axis is created by a vista, *i.e.*, by the eye's looking through or down an opening, a frame, or at a motive of decoration. Then a desire to see one side like the other is always sensible. There is also a constructional need of symmetry when the width of an arch ring carries one set of mouldings over to the other (as just seen in *A* and *B* of Fig. 81). But neither of these reasons exists in the case of a point. The eye cannot see through solid stone and no arch goes from one side to the other. Therefore, there is no inherent reason why one side of a point or wall, or any piece of poché, should be like the other side. The axis of symmetry of a point is, in essence, a meaningless term.

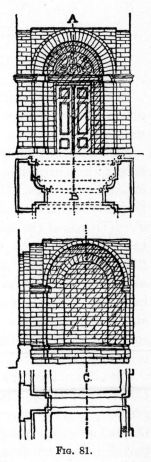

FIG. 81.

What then is the origin of the form of words, "a

P

symmetrical point," and why should we also, by way of paradox, speak of "placing the axes" of such points? As a result of a repeated opening or motive, the two sides of the intermediate point, having a like use, have a like form. The result is a symmetrical point; but it is only a result or happening. Let us remember that the silhouette of a piece of poché depends upon the motive which is framed in, and that when the two motives on each side of the poché are unlike, the two sides of the point will be different. In practice, if a wall is much cut into on one side, for the sake of good construction, and therefore of good planning, it is better to keep it quite plain on the other.

The study of the silhouette of poché is not all that an architect has to think about. Even more important is the question of its size or weight. The different walls and points of a large plan are by no means the same size. A glance at one of the plans in the foregoing pages shows this. Here by half closing our eyes, or by putting them slightly out of focus, we become conscious of interior suites of heavier walls. These predominant lines are "interior silhouettes" and should make a closed line; the eye should be able to follow such a line, back to the starting point, through the different convolutions to which it may be subjected. This is as true as that each room should be closed; the reason will be apparent when we have studied the need for varying thickness in walls.

There are four conditions to which walls, as regards their weight, must conform.

1. *The higher the wall, the thicker.*

2. *The larger the space enclosed, the thicker the wall.*

3. *When a lateral pressure occurs, the wall or point must be thicker and heavier in the line of the thrust and in proportion to it.*

4. *The material of which a wall or point is constructed will determine the class to which it belongs, and thus govern its weight.*

In independent points, the kind of construction which unites them overhead will determine their spacing, and thus, indirectly, as seen in the second condition, their size.

As the more important rooms and halls of a plan are necessarily larger and usually higher, they are marked in a plan by heavier walls. Hence the interior silhouettes just alluded to. These suites of heavier walls would only be interrupted by an introduction of new material, an unusual occurrence.

The better the grouping of a plan, the more are different interior silhouettes brought together into one suite and simplified. From this we realize a quality of impression, to be looked for in designs.

The façade walls are usually heavier than the less important interior walls and give a closed exterior silhouette.

That the shape and size of points should be materially altered by the introduction of arches and vaulting is an ABC of architecture. Nearly every student of architecture, if he has not read Ruskin, has at least been preached at by the lover of Gothic. In consequence, if he is endowed with even slight desire to learn something more than what lies on the surface, he has gone to Mr. Moore's excellent work on the Gothic construction and has perhaps made some study of Viollet le Duc and the actual buildings. If he has thus grasped the underlying principles of Gothic he will be able to use in a logical manner not merely ogives and groined vaults, but any vault. He will have learned that Gothic architects were not merely builders of pointed arches, but rather master thinkers, and he will try to follow in their footsteps. When, for the sake of character, adaptability, ease of construction, unity of decoration, style, or any other well founded reason, he chooses to introduce a barrel vault into his modern work, he will indicate heavy walls on the sides and a lighter, or even none, at the end; if a cloister vault, heavy walls on all four sides; a dome without penetrations, again a wall of uniform thickness; a groined vault, points resisting in the direction of the diagonals, or at least points which, taken together, will sum up such a resistance; a barrel, cloister or dome with penetrations, points which in their length make up for the gathering of the thrusts. In an arcade the points between arches, where thrusts annul each other, would be slight in comparison to the end point, which acts as buttress. Hence he would never end an arcade with an isolated column, but would always engage the column in a pier.

A barrel vault with, or, even better, without, penetrations, is especially appropriate for a gallery or straight staircase, or for a long hall with entrance at one end. The vertical half circle at the end offers an especially good ground for decorations to which the whole arrangement of the vault and hall leads.

A cloister vault is well adapted to a room or to an "escalier à la Française," but looks lower than does a groined vault or vault with penetrations. Domes without penetrations have a tendency to look bare, and are difficult to decorate.

Coming back to our fourth condition: as regards size of points, the difference between slight partitions or framework, brick and stone should be evident. But between any of the former and an indication of iron construction even greater difference should exist. All this must be felt in the plan as much as in elevation. To give such indication correctly the student must acquaint himself with the dimensions of each material and depict an honest use.

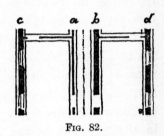

FIG. 82.

Having reviewed the general laws which may be said to govern indication of poché, let us take up several cases and add a few suggestions as to the means of giving scale.

First, two parallel walls near together should not usually, unless both are as thin as possible, be of the same thickness. In Fig. 82 *a* and *b* would be unlike, the floor beams carrying from *c* to *b* and from *b* to *d* dispensing with the support of *a*. It is only in six-inch framework that the walls are of uniform thickness. One can *a priori* decide that there is probably a fault somewhere, when a plan presents the monotonous aspect induced by uniform weight of walls.

Second, for the sake of good construction, except

in unusual cases, all walls ought to go down, at least through arched piers, to the foundations. Only thin partitions should be supported on floors or by beams from pier to pier. It is perfectly evident that heavy walls can be carried across wide openings, but this is bad architecture. On the one hand is the alternative of a high steel beam. This is both expensive and heavy, unsightly from below, appears to sag with an ugly drop, may vibrate more or less and perhaps crack the decoration. Moreover, if it shows the immense weight above, (as in a façade) the beholder must unconsciously fear for its security, and a most inartistic effect will result.

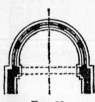

FIG. 83.

On the other hand, a little more serious study is necessary to arrange the plan so that the wall may be supported on solid arching or be built up from the ground.

A possible fault of this kind is that exhibited when the façade wall of an upper story is built across above the end of a room having a circular extension, without an arch to support it (Fig. 83). Naturally, if an arch is used, the diameter of the circular plan cannot be very great. As a rule, all holes, windows, doors, bays, etc., should be kept one above the other; thus the points will also be over each other.

Another arrangement that is good or bad for constructive reasons is the Palladian motive. This should only be used between piers or when slightly set back from a façade (Fig. 84). The suggestion of a thrust from the arch needs these lateral buttresses to make it seem secure. Palladio and the old Italians always used it thus, and modern students cannot do better than imitate their work as shown in the Villa Medici of Rome.

As said under "Optical Effects," all reëntrant circles in plan should have their centers set back. When indicating columns in plan keep in mind that those of the same height would have approximately the same diameter. Columns may be either engaged from one third to one quarter or disengaged, providing the distance from the pier to the column is not equal to the latter's diameter. They should never be tangent or almost tangent. The grouping together of four columns, sometimes seen in German plans, is not often successful. A super-

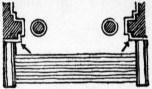

Fig. 84.

fluity of columns is to be avoided. This superfluity can be detected in impression by the plan looking like a pool table full of billiard balls. In execution such prodigality gives to the confused beholder the sensation of being in an unordered forest of tree trunks. It is well to place a corresponding pilaster behind a disengaged column (Fig. 85) to hold up the inner end of the entablature (at a). One may deduce a rule from this: that an entablature should always have a support at its end or turning.

We have not yet spoken of the dancing of stairs, although it is a subject that might have been included in earlier chapters. In America, a corner in a staircase is usually turned by brutally running each step

FIG. 85.

to the center; and later on, when the staircase is found dangerous, the architect contents himself with condemning all winding staircases. Such turns, however, would be perfectly easy and safe if properly made, the principle being to progressively increase and then decrease the widths of the steps measured on an outer circle. Thus persons going up or down are not confronted with a sudden change in length of the step necessary, and unconsciously accommodate themselves. Other advantages of dancing the steps are that the hand-rail does not follow a broken curve, and that, inasmuch as the change of width is begun before reaching the turn, reduced portions of the steps at the turn are actually broader, while broader portions are narrower. M. Pillet in his "Stéréotomie" gives the two best mechanical methods for dancing steps, but it seems even better to do this by eye.

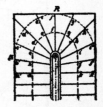

FIG. 86.

Just as a hand-made curve is always superior to a constructed curve, so will the free dancing be to the more mathematical. As in Fig. 86, we take our line of construction a, b, c about twenty inches from the hand-rail and, realizing that a step in the axis R would be symmetrically affected, are able to use it as a starting point. We next lay off our treads at f, e, d, c, b, a and $f, g, h, i, j, k,$ a and k being the first steps we have decided to make straight. The dancing must not be carried too far, as the steps would become too much inclined to the direction of passage. Through a point taken on a wider circle, R, S (center o), we draw our first corrected step in such a way that $a', b',$ etc., will be increased till R is reached, and then decrease progressively. The architect must try for a gradual alteration of direction which presents no sudden change, and he recorrects the lines $aa', bb', cc',$ etc., just as he would the breaks in a freehand curve.

In order to give scale to points, we have recourse to

the laws enumerated in Part II. An element more or less definite in deciding the scale of a plan, where a truss construction is used for the roofing, etc., is the spacing of the points themselves. The ordinary distances between axes of successive points of poché in a wall which is to support trusses, would be from twelve to fifteen feet. In large trusses this is increased.

Another thing to remember in planning the interior decoration of a room is that single 45° motives in the corner (A, Fig. 87) will always give less scale than two motives (such as B of the same figure). It is quite difficult to obtain much scale with a 45° motive. The only successful way is to introduce sub-elements, decorative columns, statues, etc., and run the risk of becoming complicated and perhaps of being, even then, unable to prevent these elements from seeming additions in miniature, themselves out of scale.

FIG. 87.

In modern planning, one of the best examples of carefully studied points and arrangement of a difficult disposition of axes, brought together and made clear, is a plan already shown, M. Pascal's Grand Prix (Fig. 23). This design is for three distinct but communicating private hotels, belonging to the same family, and is for an irregular piece of ground.

INDICATION OF MOSAIC

The mosaic of a plan (we are now speaking of exhibition work) is intended to define and characterize qualities already existent in the poché; to intensify the architect's interpretation of the program, and to aid in interpreting his own ideas. This being the case, it hardly seems a mistake to allow the introduction of mosaic in competition drawings, despite contrary opinion. What is aimed at in competitive work is a comparison of the ideas of different architects. It has been urged against the rendering and mosaicing of such work that these "tricks" catch the eye and make a poor plan look better than its neighbors. But such assertions must have been made by men who did not understand the reading of mosaic. In reality, unless the rendering of a plan does carry out the thought of which the poché is the expression, if it is put in at random, it would much better be altogether omitted. If the labels on the bottles in an apothecary's shop are mixed, more harm is likely to ensue than if the different poisons were left unlabeled. At least, then, the skilled chemist would not be led to use prussic acid for distilled water.

From this we may deduce that mosaic must, above all, be characteristic. Since it is to act as a label only, it must never be dark enough to detract from the poché, to clutter up the plan. Interior mosaic may be made somewhat more intricate, and thus on the whole darker than exterior mosaic, but should be done with a finer line. Moreover, when the design contains many repeated lines, these should be in a lighter ink. Light washes may be used to bring out the design of interior work or to express different kinds of mosaic, furniture, etc., but the lighter and more monochrome such washes, the better. In the rendering of exteriors, it is also true that dark tones and varied colors are bad. The poché should shine out in the plan, should predominate and make the first impression.

For this reason a base line or "ligne de retraite" of light ink is drawn around all the poché, about a millimeter from it in interior work and on the exterior as much as two millimeters. These distances, however, vary with the scale of the plan. No washes or mosaic should cross this base line. Observance of this will leave the poché free and give brilliancy. Usually a very light gray wash is put all over the exterior of a plan, in order to leave the buildings light and give them prominence. This wash should be little more than dirty water. All the washes of a plan are usually graded from top to bottom. The shadows are cast from the upper left-hand corner. The latter are best left out, unless there is considerable exterior work, gardening and terracing, which need explanation. Some years ago the custom of grading a tone over staircases prevailed, but this usually makes a spot which attracts undue attention, and may be dispensed with.

As to optical illusions, resulting from the introduction of mosaic (see also the chapter on Optical Effects, page 141), space (room, hall or gallery, etc.) left quite white naturally attracts more attention and appears larger than the same space made gray by wash. A design that has no definite personal divisions in its composition but gives an even gray tone and runs to the base line makes a space count for its

Fig. 88. — 1re 2me Grand Prix by M. Bigot. "Une École Supérieure de Marine."

full size; this is true, too, of a design that grades
evenly from gray at the base line to light or white in
the middle. On the contrary, if there are introduced
distinctive divisions, dark in the middle, with a decided white band between center design and poché,
or a greater number of dissimilar dark and light bands,
the whole space seems reduced.

Contrasts will always count; that is, in a light
plan the principal motives should be treated with a
darker design, or, if the whole be covered with lines,
a darker or very light, perhaps quite white, treatment
will be proper for the climax. The climax must have
the richest or most interesting mosaic. In a white
treatment this can be attained by arranging a brilliant and sparkling composition, as a border or fringe,
gray at the base line, grading to white.

If a repetition of parallel lines or small spaces, etc.,
is used, the whole must be kept absolutely even and
regular, for the slightest irregularity in such a tone
attracts attention; a rubber is useful in equalizing
faulty portions. The use of a light gray wash is
often better than such pen-work imitation of the en-
graver.

We may distinguish three distinct kinds of interior
mosaic:

(1) that which shows the flooring and is projected
up;

(2) that which shows objects in the plan, furniture,
etc., and is projected up;

(3) that which shows the ceiling or vaulting and is
projected down.

It sometimes happens that all three kinds of mosaic are used in the same plan. The first two may be shown in one room, the groundwork to disappear under the furniture. A needful explanation might even be given by projecting the constructive lines of a ceiling (penetrations, etc.), drawn in dotted or full lines on top of the first two picturings; but it is difficult to keep such drawings clear. It is more customary, expecially in plans of upper floors, to characterize salons and other rooms with interesting ceilings by indication of these decorations, reserving the first two methods for less important places.

While the second and third methods should actually conform to the practical exigencies of a plan, the first may be more or less conventional, and merely give the character of the flooring (stone, cement, wood, etc.). Ordinarily, no attempt is made to draw in a number of boards, which would but blacken the plan and destroy all effects of the poché.

The mosaic which most effectually characterizes a plan is that of the second method. An example is M. Bigot's plan (Fig. 88), with its excellent portrayal of batteries, machines and implements for cadet drill. As a rule, all passages and circulations should be left white, or only with a border line. M. Chaussemiche's plan (Fig. 70) shows this particularly well. Moreover, lines must not cross an opening where a passage is to count. This is apparent in the entrance to M. Chaussemiche's plan, and a clever breaking of the mosaic of the broad gallery around his central court gives an excellent example of one method of tying the

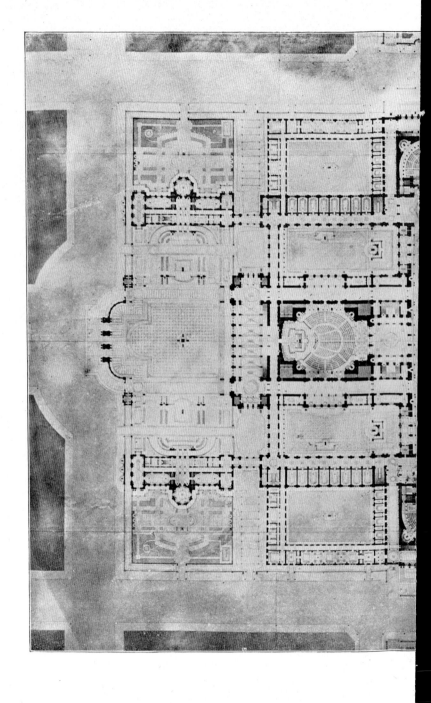

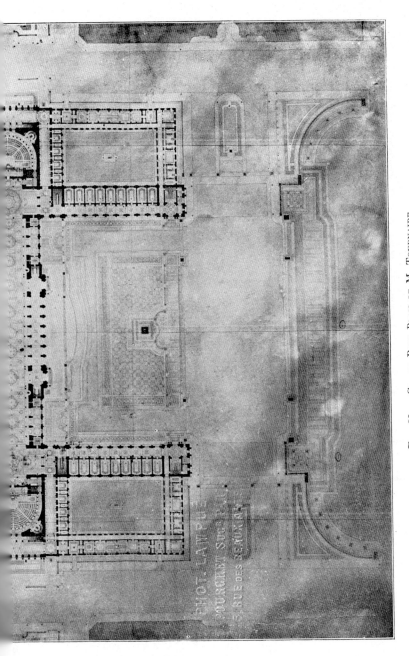

Fig. 89.—Grand Prix Plan of M. Tournaire.

central spaces to those portions with which it should be in direct communication. Indeed, the mosaic in this plan will well repay careful study.

For exterior work, a most characteristic court mosaic can be made by using the old Roman Opus Insertum, or a flagging laid in and bonded as a wall would be. As with repetitions of parallel lines, great care must be taken that the effect is regular, and not dark in spots.

There is a last remark applicable to the designing of decoration, poché and mosaic alike. It has to do with repeated motives; there are examples in both M. Chaussemiche's and M. Tournaire's Grand Prix. Successive groups of similar repeated motives, having not less than five elements in each group, will seem equal, although there may be slight differences in the actual number of elements. That is to say, in Fig. 70 we see a side elevation of three apparently equal divisions; but counting the number of windows, we find that the last division has six windows in its length, while each of the others has but five. Likewise, in Fig. 89 two courts balance each other as regards the main lateral axis; yet the arcades which compose them differ in number. There is no mathematical rule in art. That which looks right is right.

To sum up, both poché and mosaic should be characteristic, rich and interesting in the important parts of the plan; more simple in the others; and the mosaic should unite the plan, accentuate the passages and bring out the grouping decided on for the poché.

PART VI

CHAPTER I

PRACTICAL SUGGESTIONS IN PLANNING

As in foregoing parts of this discussion, limited space will only allow us a few suggestions as to practical needs of different kinds of buildings. Each program must be so unlike all other programs that a separate treatise on each possible subject would be necessary to cover the ground. Moreover, needs change with times, and what might be laid down to-day, in a few years would become useless. Every program must, of necessity, receive especial study from the practical point of view, a task which the individual architect performs for himself. Only the most general classing, then, is within the province of this discussion. Be it remembered, the following recommendations are not given as absolute.

THE HOUSE

Any distinct sketch of the domestic architecture of times past, or even of domestic architecture and needs in foreign countries to-day, would take much time and be of little use. It is, therefore, best to limit the field to our own time and country, the twentieth century and America. I remember some excellent re-

marks made by an American architect who has had
great success in domestic work, and which will serve
as introduction to the present subject. He said that
a house, the home of a man and of his family, should
be, primarily, an expression of the character of its
inmates. The first duty of the architect who wants
to make a suitable abode for some one else is not
merely to study the requirements that are laid before him on paper, but to acquaint himself with the
habits and tastes of the people whose abode he is to
build. A man who wants to splurge — not only to
entertain, but to show that he can entertain — should
not be housed in a brown Quaker-like cottage any
more than the quiet student in a casino or café-concert.

Not that any artist should do violence to his tastes
and become vulgar. That would be as false as to do
violence to his client's characteristics. Shakespeare
was always Shakespeare, whether he was interpreting
a Falstaff, a Richard the Third or a Rosalind. The
architect, however, must not build his own house and
then expect every one to be happy therein. He should
read his client, and translate the reading into wood
and stone. So doing, he will unconsciously carry
out the aim of another successful man, who said:
"Each house should have some especial arrangement,
some new problem worked out and expressed in it."
No two human beings are alike, and if the houses they
inhabit are characteristic of them the houses will be
unlike. Thus the architect of the houses will never
hear the reproach, "Oh yes, that was built by Smith.
All his designs are the same."

Q

As to general requirements of modern life in America, in the placing of any house there are to be considered : approach, possible views from the house, orientation and prevailing local winds. The kitchens must not be apparent from the approach; the living and reception rooms must profit by the view; breakfast rooms, etc., should face east; bedrooms and living rooms not restricted to a north exposure; porches verandas, etc., toward the view on the sunny side of the house and protected from the wind. In a warm climate or for summer it is well to have a north porch, shielded from the rays of the hot sun; in a cold climate, the entrance door should not be on the north side of the house; the kitchen, because usually too warm, may well face north.

Then comes the question whether or not a client intends to entertain much. If he does, the house should "open up" well; rooms be large, and connected by wide doorways; salons carefully placed "en suite," in order to obtain as many vistas as possible. If not for entertaining, the rooms may be smaller and not necessarily so connected. In that case prominence should be given to the minor arrangements, fireplaces, with seats, nooks, etc., and a more homelike and domestic atmosphere diffused through the work.

In general, there are three groupings in the program of a modern North American habitation : First, rooms affected especially by the family; second, those for the reception and entertainment of strangers; third, those given over to the servants. It will not be easy to discuss each group separately, but the reader should bear in mind that in making a design he must not allow one group to interfere with another. By way of illustration, in the average well-devised house there ought to be two staircases, one for the family and visitors, and another for the servants; there should be not less than three bathrooms, one connected with the guest rooms, one for the family, and a separate one for the servants.

' To take up in order the requisites of a house: the entrance hall should be preceded by a vestibule seconded by a cloak room or cloak closet, and a toilet room may well be another adjunct. The entrance hall must permit of necessary furniture. As intimated, in a house destined for entertaining, the salons should be in succession, giving vistas and suites of perspective; small salons, etc., at the end of the large ones; never a small one between two large ones; reception rooms at the entrance of the house. In rooms for official or public receptions, a double (parallel) circulation through the rooms must be planned. Ball rooms should have provision for the orchestra.

In a library, the two requirements are wall-space for the bookcases and light for reading. One end might be given over to bookcases and the other with a fireplace, to study. Excessive heat is bad for the books; hence book shelves must never quite reach to the top of the room. Dens and smoking rooms should be comfortably furnished with nooks and fireplaces; it is well to place a toilet room near. In a billiard room, allow six feet of free space around the billiard table. A raised platform for onlookers is good (extra space). Light from two sides is needed to obviate direct shadows.

Dining rooms, on the east side of the house, should be long rather than square, not less than 13 feet 6 inches in any direction (extra allowance being made when furniture subtracts from this dimension.) Provision is to be made for the sideboard. The best place for the fireplace is usually at the end of the room, so placed as not to scorch those at table. Cross lights are good in a dining room; otherwise light from end, that one person only need have light directly in front or light directly behind.

A butler's pantry should communicate with both dining room and kitchen, but in such a way as not to become merely a passage from one to the other. The butler's pantry must be at least five by eight feet and ought to contain a sink (hot and cold water), shelves and cases for china, etc. In a well-planned house there will be an ice box, with compartments for food, opening, one from the butler's pantry, one from the kitchen, while the portion reserved for the ice itself opens from a side porch or outer kitchen. Last in the list of pantries should be a light kitchen closet or kitchen pantry, with space for flour barrels.

Kitchens must be well lighted, and, as before suggested, may be placed on the north side of the house. The range and hot water boiler are not to be near the kitchen table and sink, for in summer, proximity of either makes it impossible to work. All plumbing should be kept away from outside walls, but the sink put near a window. It is important to place a hood with a vent not smaller than 12″ × 17″ over the range or stove. The proper finish for a kitchen is paint or tiles. A tile floor might, however, be too cold. "Composition" makes a good substitute. Laundries should have well-lighted stationary tubs, the plumbing kept away from outside walls. A drying room with stove is an excellent addition. The back stairs of a house ought never to open directly out of the kitchen; if they do they form a sort of chimney, drawing all the odors of cooking to the upper floors. It is becoming more and more necessary to plan servants' dining rooms or sitting rooms in our modern houses. These can only be dispensed with when the kitchen is very large and there is a sewing room upstairs where servants may sit.

On the upper floors bedrooms naturally form the important feature. Here care must be taken to allow room for different pieces of necessary furniture. Beds should never be placed in a draught, nor so disposed that light from the window will shine directly into the eyes of the occupant. Artificial lights are required at each side of the dressing tables. Planning of the children's rooms should permit the mother of the family to come from her own chamber to the children without passing through the general hall. Guest rooms should not open so as to command those of the family.

Dressing rooms need to be well lighted and heated, connected with the bedrooms to which they belong and have a separate entrance, in order that a maid or valet can prepare toilet arrangements. In a large house it is well to plan a bathroom for each bedroom. Bathrooms should not have more than one entrance, unless exception be made for separate entrances, exclusively for a servant who is to prepare the bath, etc. The best arrangement is a small vestibule leading from both bedroom and hall and into the bathroom. Proper finishes for the last are paint, putty, tiles, or some similar washable substance. Bathrooms and toilet rooms in any house should be so disposed that plumbing may be kept in vertical line. Soil and waste pipes must not be visible, but accessible in case of need.

Bed and bath rooms ought never to be too near the servants' staircases, or arranged so that the noise or inopportune presence of servants coming down in the morning may be annoying. If possible, arrange that the servants' staircase may be entirely closed off from the part of the house given over to family sleeping rooms. This is a sure way to avoid the numerous annoyances, inevitable if servants must pass through the main hall of the house. In any case, make back stair landings independent of all lower passages. Linen closets, and sewing room next it, have as chief requisite good light.

All the windows of a house, indeed those of most buildings, should reach the ceiling. This will force a change of air in the upper parts of the rooms.

STABLES

Remember that horses, if not human beings, are yet beings. They require plenty of air, protection from sudden changes of temperature and a dry place in which to live. Stables are better if opening south and built of stone or brick with tile flooring or cement treated with oxide of iron. Wood, because it does not dry, makes poor flooring; it has, though, an advantage over stone for stalls, as the latter may cause injury to a stamping horse. An inclined waterproof concrete floor with level removable oak slat floor on top is good. Enamelled brick protected by wood kicking boards makes a good lining of stalls, indeed of the whole stable. Brick opposite the horse's eyes should not be white. Rafters of a stable should not project down or be

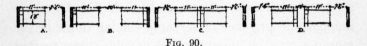

FIG. 90.

apparent to make corners for the accumulation of dust. The ground of the stalls, etc., must have an inclination of $2\frac{1}{2}$ or 3 per cent., to allow the water to run off, and the gutter 2 per cent. Too great height of ceiling in a stable is bad, since the floor will remain badly heated. Stalls should not be less than nine feet high in the clear on account of possible accident to rearing horses. Carriage rooms about twelve feet high. The windows should be placed high, and, because of draughts, are best behind the horses. In each stable the man's room should be placed so as to enable him to have oversight of the horses at night. The best plan is to place it at the end of a rectangular stable, raising the room floor three or four feet, that a window will overlook the stalls.

Figure 90 gives different arrangements of stalls in a

stable. In A windows can easily be placed behind the horses. The width of the passage may be somewhat reduced; but it is well to have room to turn a horse. In B, if the stable is short, windows would be placed at each end to give light down the central passage; if the stable is long, they must be placed in the walls at the heads of the horses, high and possibly opposite the partitions. C is the best arrangement. The horses can see each other, and the draught question is easily solved. D is a last, rather luxurious, disposition. It is not certain that the central passage made for the groom is a very good addition; for thus the horses grow less accustomed to having him enter the stalls.

Following are some dimensions adopted for cavalry stables in France. The partitions between the stalls are kept low. The minimum cube of air necessary for each horse is 20 mc.

Width of stall, 1.45 m.
Width of stable, one row of horses, 6 m.
Width of stable, two rows of horses and passage, 10.40 m.
Width of stable, two rows, head to head, 12 m.
Height of ceiling, 3.50 m.

Calculating the cube of air for each of these, we find, respectively, 30.45 m., 26.39 m. and 30.45 m.

The hay is stored above the stable and can thus be let down to each horse through traps. For the manure hole, ten cubic feet is enough per horse, if the manure is taken away every day. No manure should be left against a wall of the stable, because the cement or mortar would be corroded.

An adjunct of stables is the court for cleaning horses. This must be open on a side other than the north.

In carriage houses it must be possible to wheel each carriage, without turning, into its respective place. No vehicle should be in front of another. In other words, the ideal carriage house is a rectangular room as long as the sum of the widths of the carriages to be stored, about eighteen feet wide, with a door eight feet wide in front of the place of each carriage. It is well to allow ten feet as the width of each carriage, although it is possible to do with less.

Harness rooms should be cool and dry; harness not kept in the stables.

BUILDINGS FOR COMMUNITIES

In all buildings where an agglomeration of persons live together, among the chief needs are assured cleanliness and good ventilation.

In barrack buildings the windows should be as high as possible, with low sills, and there should be at least 450 cubic feet of air per soldier in the barrack room. All interior reëntrant angles or corners are to be rounded out, and no projections allowed to make unnecessary angles. Horses are not to be put under any part of such buildings.

In the study of homes and retreats for the aged, infirm or incurable, no matter what the practical exigencies, the architect should seek to produce, as much as possible, the aspect or illusion of the individual home. As far as may be, everything which tends to prolong life, to make it gay and bright, is to be supplied.

As later to be observed, this is equally true in the case of insane asylums.

When dormitories exist, they should not be too long — sixteen to twenty beds is a maximum. Staircases, in short flights, with intermediary landings, no turning stairs. Elevators supplement the stairs. The windows of the dormitories ought to be four feet wide, and on both sides of the room, to give good ventilation; ceilings sixteen to twenty feet high; width of rooms twenty-five to thirty feet, for children, twenty-two feet. Rooms should be finished with oil paint or with some similar washable substance; but the floors of hard wood should be waxed, never washed; otherwise they retain moisture and give rise to dampness. Floors covered with linoleum can be mopped.

It is not necessarily advisable to place dining halls near the dormitories; never kitchens near the latter, although these should communicate with the dining halls. The best arrangement for dining halls is that of small tables of six to ten places each.

There should always be an infirmary connected with a home or retreat, and here the dormitory must have 2,000 to 3,000 cubic feet of air per patient.

HOSPITALS

The same need of giving as much pleasure as possible to the inmates felt in designing a home or retreat is present in planning a hospital. Great simplicity is also necessary here. Corners and projections make receptacles for dust; dust and dirt are the home of microbes. In the plan for a hospital there must be no closed courts, no reëntrant angles between buildings — in the ideal, no joining whatever, each building quite separate and only united to the others by low or open galleries.

Orientation, being governed by atmospheric conditions, varies with the place. Usually the longest side of a building is placed across the direction of the prevailing wind, thus insuring the greatest possibility of a constant change of air. All the buildings of one hospital would, naturally, lie in the same direction. Two or three stories are admissible.

Windows of wards need not be wide, but should be high and rise to the ceiling, the sills about three feet six inches from the floor. There should be a small opening at the floor level to permit of occasional thorough ventilation there. The beds of the patients are best placed with the head toward the wall between windows; but it is advisable to leave a small space or passage between head of bed and wall. There should be but one bed between two windows. Width of room would be from twenty-five to twenty-eight feet; of a window, about three feet eight inches, and of wall space between windows, five feet four inches — in all nine feet from axis to axis of windows. The *minimum* cube of air for each patient is from 1,800 to 2,000 cubic feet. This gives as height between ceiling and floor sixteen feet. No curtains or hangings are allowed in a hospital. All angles are to be rounded out, the walls covered with paint or some similar washable substance, the floors of oak with paraffine finish and all cracks kept carefully filled, or of linoleum cemented down.

If chutes are installed, two are necessary from each ward to the basement; one for clothes to be washed, and the other for cloths, etc., to be destroyed. Many authorities question the advisability of chutes, as they raise infected dust at the bottom.

Open fireplaces are good additions to the heating and ventilation. These are especially salutary because they give a cheerful aspect to the sick room, and so improve the mental tone of the patients. Of course, there must be a carefully regulated heating apparatus.

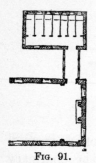

FIG. 91.

The stairs, short, straight flights, with two or three platforms between stories, are supplemented by elevators with room for a stretcher. Water closets, having ventilation from at least two sides, are to be placed at an exterior angle of the building or, better yet, entirely separated therefrom and connected by low passages (Fig. 91). For the bathrooms a special program should be exacted. Vaulted rooms are good here, because the vapor that is sure to condense will run down the sides, and can be collected at the floor level.

Small wards for contagious diseases, recognized too late, ought to exist in all hospitals.

In surgical hospitals the passages must be arranged so as to avoid sudden turns in transporting a patient from his ward to the operating room. Sudden turns produce shocks and consequent pain. The operating room must have vertical as well as horizontal light; no projections; corners rounded out, and walls so treated as to allow of thorough disinfecting.

In hospitals for contagious diseases, make many small wards. Since it is never allowable to pass through one ward to reach another, a separate passage or access is necessary. As the open air treatment gains ground the program for hospital planning is being greatly modified. In order to care for uncovered patients means of temporarily placing the bed in a warmed space must be devised. Porches should not be over twelve feet deep: the architect must keep in mind that sunlight as well as free circulation of air is all important.

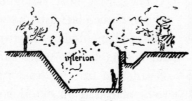

interior

FIG. 92.

There are numberless accessories for a hospital which must have a special program. The pharmacy is best placed on the ground floor, that it may dispose of a cool basement for perishable substances. Sound of the machinery should never be perceptible from the wards. Also, all depressing sights, funeral arrangements, etc., are to be kept away from the patients. For each ward, provide a diet kitchen in direct communication by dumb waiter, etc., with the main kitchen.

In insane asylums there are different groups of patients to be separated. The cries of turbulent patients should not be audible to excite the more quiet. An asylum must be more or less a prison, but without evidence thereof. There are usually more women than men, therefore a symmetrical composition balancing the quarters of the two sexes is not possible.

The gardens ought to be large and attractive; yet arranged to facilitate surveillance. Rocks or ponds, which might promote suicides, all possible causes of accident, should be excluded; even locks, sunk in the doors. Walls around the asylum, if sunk, as in Fig. 92, allow patients to look out over the country, and so lessen the feeling of restraint.

SCHOOLS

Taking up the question of schools, we find different categories of rooms and courts. The latter should never be closed on all four sides, and one of the open sides should not be toward the north. This is to assure sunshine in the court, that the latter may be completely dried.

Dining rooms in school buildings are to be lighted, if possible, on both sides; kitchens separated from living, study and class rooms; study rooms and bedrooms or dormitories arranged so sun enters during the day. Light for study or class rooms is to come from the left of the student, and never from behind a lecturer or speaker. It is not well to make these rooms more than twenty-five feet wide, for even with very large windows the light, in sufficient quantity, will not penetrate to a greater depth. A usual rule is to make the glass area in windows equal to between twenty and twenty-five per cent. of the floor area of the classroom. Piers should not be more than three feet wide from a cross wall, nor than about five feet between windows. Windows must always go to the ceiling, and sills are made about three feet high. The sill is not made much higher — it would cast a shadow on the workers. A room for lessons in mathematics and other subjects necessitating blackboard must not exceed in length twenty-eight or thirty feet — figures are not legible at greater distance. Open air and low temperature schools are gaining approval, and here a requisite is the possibility of cross ventilation.

In open air schools plan class rooms to eliminate sound communications or screen the windows to catch the sound waves, yet leave the full area unreduced for ventilation. Hot water heating systems in open buildings mean bursting radiators.

BUILDINGS FOR HIGHER INSTRUCTION

Universities and Colleges, etc.
Amphitheaters and Lecture Halls

In such halls never make unnecessarily wide passages. The audience ought to be placed in a room of the minimum size, to obviate effort in hearing, seeing and speaking. Roughly, it is allowable to count two and one half persons to ten square feet of floor area, including passages and allowing each person an auditorium chair for writing. This is a maximum for a large hall; in a small hall where a generous treatment is desired, only two persons to ten or twelve square feet should be counted. (The smaller the hall, the larger in proportion becomes the space appropriated by the passages and platform.)

A serious course of lectures cannot adequately be given to an audience of more than 500 or 600 people; for a larger number the size of the hall becomes too great, and those on the outskirts will find difficulty in hearing and seeing. This, naturally, does not apply to popular lectures, nor, *a fortiori*, to halls where the question in hand is to be treated in a merely oratorical manner. The amphitheater, semicircular in plan, is adapted to the hearing of an orator. The amphitheater is advantageous in that it places a maximum number of persons near the speaker, but faulty because hard to place in plan, to roof, light and divide as to aisles and entrances. It should be reserved for an audience of 250 persons or more. Using the formula

$$R = \sqrt{\frac{2\,a}{\pi}}$$

where a is the floor area, we find that, allowing two persons to ten square feet,

$$R = \sqrt{\frac{2 \times 2500}{\pi \times 2}} = \sqrt{\frac{2500}{3.14}} = \sqrt{796} = \text{about 28 ft. 3 in.}$$

An amphitheater smaller than this (for here we have allowed a generous spacing of seats and not counted the distance to the tympanum wall) would hardly be possible. A rational minimum might be a radius of twenty-five feet; fifty feet diameter. For audiences of less than 250 persons, use a rectangular hall, with seats arranged on a curve.

Halls for scientific courses requiring a blackboard

must always be rectangular and the benches or seats in a straight or slightly curved line. This is because the line of vision must, necessarily, remain perpendicular to the blackboard. In a physics lecture hall the laboratory is often placed behind the hall, and a sliding partition finished with a blackboard closes a wide opening and hides an experiment table and furnace hood. The as-

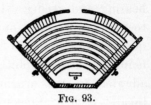

FIG. 93.

sistant in the laboratory can thus prepare experiments during the explanation; later the professor opens the sliding screen to perform the experiment. Physics requires supplementary blackboards on each side; chemical work, less blackboard space. A hall of the form shown in Fig. 93, having mirrors on the surfaces a and b, may be placed at 45° in the angle of a plan. The mirrors show experiments from the side.

There is a specially arranged hall in the Sorbonne for the observation of experiments in vivisection. The operator stands at the bottom, in the center of a series of raised circular platforms; on these latter the students, one tier above another, leaning upon rails that curve slightly over (Fig. 94). The condi-

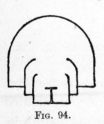

FIG. 94.

tions are that the eye of the spectator shall not be more than eight feet from the operation. The operator, who works on a pivoting table, is really at the bottom of an inverted cone, or rather at the center of a hemisphere of heads. Forty or fifty students can thus

R

observe an operation. Being only in the hall for a short time they do not need to take notes.

To prevent crowding, all large halls should have a number of entrances or exits. Gallery staircases should never be inside the hall, because of the disturbance caused by late arrivals. Staircases that are to serve as exits from public gatherings ought not to have any winding stairs; in a crowd, those on the inside near the rail might be thrown down. Several moderately wide staircases are better than a few very wide ones, unless straight flights succeed each other in the same direction. This, because a broad stream of people, turning a corner, becomes jammed toward the inside.

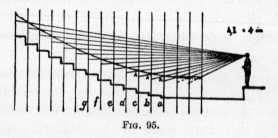

FIG. 95.

In the arrangement of the seats of a hall there should be no long rows or benches, for places in the middle are difficult of access. Seven seats from an aisle is a limit. Fig. 95 shows a method for determining the respective levels of seats in a hall. The verticals a, b, c, d, e, etc., are equally spaced; the ray from the eye of each spectator is made to pass at the same height (four inches, perhaps) above the head of the spectator directly in front. This gives a curve for the locus of the points representing the eyes of the spectators.

Lighting exclusively from above is unsuited to lecture halls; moreover, it does not permit a quick change of air between lectures, so is reprehensible in point of ventilation. The best light is from three sides, especially for blackboard work; light from behind the lecturer is inadmissible. If light is unilateral it must come from the left of the spectators. This is permissible when the height of the room is equal or greater than two thirds of the width, the latter not being excessive, say less than thirty or thirty-five feet. Windows rise to the ceiling and sills are not more than three feet six inches high. There should be a great many windows with no wide wall spaces between. Artificial light is to be diffused. A central chandelier is not good. For lantern and stereoscopic work automatically closing windows are best.

The question of acoustics is of the utmost importance. So many factors, uncontrollable by the architect, enter into the problem (presence or absence of audience, etc.) that no definite result can be obtained. Nevertheless, it is possible to plan for usual conditions.

A sound wave, beginning at a point and spreading out into space in an even temperature, grows in a spherical form from the point of origin as center. Its intensity diminishes approximately as its surface increases; in other words, in proportion to the square of the radius. Consequently the intensity of the sound ten feet from the center would be a fourth as loud as it would be five feet thence.

But if a sound passes through a straight tube it is

held in, the intensity being diminished by the viscosity of the air, by friction, reflection and absorption from the sides of the tube. This is not very great in proportion to the distance traveled. A megaphone acts somewhat like a tube in projecting sound in a certain direction. Indeed, a speaker's mouth has a certain similarity to both; this explains the indistinctness of the voice heard from behind the speaker.

Therefore, as to sounds that come to the hearer directly, without reflection, the hall most resembling a speaking tube gives best results; in other words, a long, narrow hall with, preferably, a barrel vault, the speaker placed at one end and the audience ranged in slightly rising rows on the floor and in balconies at the end.

But another important factor, affecting the sonority of a hall, is the reflection of the sound. A sound wave, striking against a flat, properly composed surface (a stone wall or similar reflecting substance), is reflected in seemingly almost equal intensity, the angle of reflection being equal to that of incidence. Soft substances do not reflect sound, and a much broken-up surface is less effective. For this reason a hall which, empty, produces echoes may, filled with an audience, prove acceptable.

Experiments have shown that if one sound is heard only one tenth of a second after another the two are confused and apparently form only one; a greater lapse of time, however, allows of the sounds being distinguished. Investigations confirming these figures were made for the arrangement of the amphitheaters of the new Sorbonne in Paris. It was there finally determined that if, in subtracting the distance traveled by a sound, in direct line between the point of origin and the observer, from the sum of the distances traveled over by the sound between the point of origin and the reflecting surface and between the reflecting surface and the observer, the space did not exceed thirty-four meters, no echo would be discernible.

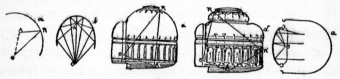

FIG. 96.

In Fig. 96, a, if $OR + RA - OA \lessgtr 34$ meters $\lessgtr 112$ feet, the sound at A will be affected in intensity, but not echoed.

It is this reënforcing of the sound which makes it absolutely necessary to displace a speaker from the center of a circular hall. He might otherwise be deafened by the reflection of his own words returning from all points at once. Indeed, a number of sound waves should not be allowed to center in one point, as the audience there would be distressed (Fig. 96, b). Moreover, in a hall for an orchestra, reflected waves from one side (for instance, that of the bass instruments) must not overbalance in certain parts of the hall, and so destroy the effect of the other instruments.

The architect must remember that sound waves are reflected more from the ceiling or dome of a hall than from the walls (c, Fig. 96), and that the same formula,

$OR + RA - OA < 112$ feet, is still to be applied. Also, double reflections may occur, and then, as in Fig. 96, d, $OR + RR' + R'A - OA \lesseqgtr 112$ feet would be the formula.

It is usually these doubly reflected sounds that exceed the limit of our formula. In consequence, they

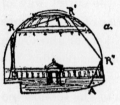

are to be guarded against. They are less likely to come from the dome than from the sides of a hall. In fact, a dome, if not too high up, nor too large, can ordinarily be counted on merely to increase the " reverberation," without giving a distinct echo; the

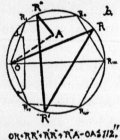

waves reflected from it must not center, and must lose themselves in the audience or a specially designed absorber (c, Fig. 96). Double reflections are likely to occur if the point of origin of the

$OR + RR' \cdot RR' + R'A - OA \lessgtr 112''$

Fig. 97.

sound is near either the prolongation of the curve of a large dome or of the walls of a cylindrical plan. Then the phenomena presented in the whispering galleries of the Capitol at Washington or the dome of St. Paul's, London, are duplicated. The sound travels along the sides of a polygon inscribed in a section of the dome or cylinder, the plane of the section being perpendicular to the reflecting surfaces, *i.e.*, passing through the center of the dome or being perpendicular to the axis of the cylinder. Fig. 97 shows in section and in plan how such repeatedly reflected sound waves may give a disastrous result. Generally speaking, all reflection of sound waves from the vertical sides of a cylindrical hall, or even of a hemicycle are to be avoided. Fig. 97, *b*, shows how the lines of the waves continue around or across a hall. Their centering or focalizing will, necessarily, create nodes or zones where it will be impossible to hear clearly. In such halls the surest way of preventing echoes is to make the seats of the audience rise well above the level of the speaker, or the origin of the sounds, and to break up, as much as possible, the vertical surfaces.

It is better not to place the origin of the sounds too far from the center of the curve of a plan, as the resultant obtuse angles of reflection nearly always lead to embarrassments. This was done in the auditorium of the Trocadero in Paris, where the plan somewhat resembles *b* of Fig. 97. Although the seats of the audience do rise above the level of the stage, the original dome sent the rising reflected waves back, and, as a result, the acoustics were so bad that a false dome had to be built inside of the real one; later on this change was supplemented by wires hung with small flags, pennants and other bits of drapery to intercept the sound waves. The last expedient was not effectual, and in certain parts of the hall it is still impossible to understand a speaker. It may be interesting to note that, although within the faulty zones a piano gives a distinct, almost unbearable, doubling of each note, organ and even orchestral music is not as noticeably bad.

The surface directly behind a speaker is usually quite unbroken, and is possibly curved forward some-

what to deflect the sound waves into a more parallel
or slightly divergent direction (see at left of c and d
of Fig. 96; also e of Fig. 96).

We have not yet discussed the manner in which the
loudness of a single prolonged note may be augmented
or decreased by interference with its reflection. If
in our formula $OR + RA - OA$ is an exact multiple
of the wave length (the distance a wave travels in a
second, about 1,100 feet, divided by the number of
vibrations per second of the particular tone) the
sound in the especial point, A, will be much augmented; on the other hand, if $OR + RA - OA$ is an
odd multiple of half wave lengths the sound will be
very much lessened. It needs only a displacement of
a few feet of either A or R to pass from the maximum
to the minimum. Also, a slight change in the note
makes as great a difference. Therefore, if but one
reflection were to affect the sound the result would be
disastrous. This never happens, but a dominating
reflection from one part of the hall might occur (such
as from the rear wall of a long hall with parallel sides),
and must always be avoided in consequence.

Usually coves between the walls and a ceiling are
good. In a long hall the end opposite the origin of the
sound should be deadened to prevent directly reflected
waves from interfering with direct waves. To sum up
the whole question, reflections which do not center (are
evenly distributed) are allowable, provided they do not
give an echo. Resonance is bad, if the material which
resounds continues the sound long after the original
sound has stopped. It is especially so when (as with

the cracked sounding-board of a piano) it produces a distinguishable note or overtones of its own. Vertical surfaces are to be broken up or covered by absorbent material except just behind the origin of the sound. Unbroken domes can only be useful when not too far off. As already suggested, stone is one of the best reflectors and it does not resound much itself; because of its qualities, however, it must not be carelessly used. Wood also is somewhat absorbent, yet a fairly good reflector, and it becomes resonant when very dry and may then increase the difficulties presented by all large halls. When wood is cracked it may be very objectionable. Metals are also resonant and, if not held securely in place, liable to produce perceptible sounds. Draperies, hangings, an audience, etc., are not reflectors and do not resound. The softer a substance or material, the less resonant is it likely to be. The breaking up of surfaces lessens their reflecting power, because the sound waves are dispersed in all directions. The older a construction the more resonant it becomes, especially when there is much wood in the interior finishing.

In all of the foregoing we have not touched upon diffraction, a factor that complicates the calculation of the exact position of the sound focal points in a large hall. Suppose a sound projected in a straight line (this is approximated by the megaphone), and that it passes the corner of a building. In doing so its direction is bent so that it tends to pass around the building. Conditions similar to this are found when sound waves cut across the edge of a balcony in an auditorium, when they pass by a cornice to be reflected by a recessed

dome or when they pass over an audience in a plane
parallel to the plane of the audience and close to it.
As yet no exact data has been obtained as to the angles
of such diffraction, but it is known that they vary with
the note and that they also vary with the proximity
of the path of the sound to the corner. As under many
conditions these angles are fifteen, twenty or more
degrees, absolutely exact computation of the directions
taken by such a sound wave are not now possible. Close
approximations can be made, and this is all that is
necessary under most conditions.

Professor Wallace C. Sabine of Harvard University
has been one of the most important contributors to
the subject of acoustics. In 1900 he published a series
of articles [1] giving information about the absorbent
material necessary to the absorption of sound under
certain conditions. The less absorbent the material the
greater the quantity needed. Later [2] Professor Sabine
made experiments to extend his deductions so as to take
in all notes of the musical scale, and a still later study [3]
takes up the comparative results of placing the absorbent material at the maximum and minimum points of
sound focalization.

To sum up the subject, the selection of the absorbing
points is of utmost importance in most cases. The
architect must so plan his surfaces and the room or hall

[1] See the American Architect, New York, 1900, issues of April 7th,
April 21st, May 5th, May 12th, May 26th, June 9th and June 16th.
[2] See the Proceedings of the American Academy of Arts and
Sciences, 1906.
[3] See the Architectural Quarterly of Harvard University, March,
1912.

that as much as possible of the reflected sound will be returned to and therefore absorbed by the audience itself. Other absorbing material is only to be introduced where necessary to prevent retarded returns of sound to the audience. Avoid concentration of the reflected sound waves, else continued notes will each have marked zones of maximum and minimum intensity. These concentrations can be avoided by breaking up the reflecting surface (as coffering a ceiling); usually the surfaces need not be made absorbent.

If the problem is a complex one or the auditorium large, the architect would better call in an expert and have the points of maxima and minima calculated and the acoustics assured before the working drawings of the plans are made.

A lecture hall should have direct ventilation, even though this is supplemented by artificial means. There must be windows which can be thrown open between lectures. Artificial ventilation can be classed in two groups: either fresh air is forced

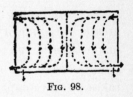

Fig. 98.

into a room, or the air of the room is drawn out. A really successful system combines these methods. If heated air is drawn or forced into a hall it must arrive at points where it will not incommode. Inlets are placed above the heads of the audience, even at the ceiling: at the latter level it spreads out, cools and is forced down to the floor. Outlets should be at the floor level and *on the same side of the room with the inlets.* This forces the air to make a circuit of the room. Fig. 98

shows how the ventilation will act, be it unilateral or bilateral.

The best way of introducing air into a room is to bring it more or less directly from the outside through a steam or, better, hot-water radiator. If the approaches to a hall are warmed, less heating will be necessary for the hall proper.

The annexes of a lecture hall are the study, or professor's room, the storage rooms, which vary in importance and size with the kind of lecture peculiar to the hall, and cloak rooms, etc.

As formerly suggested, a physical or chemical lecture hall should have laboratories, directly connected. Physical laboratories, especially, are to be furnished with vent-hoods, which must not shut off the light from work carried on beneath. The hood and laboratory table or furnace would be placed vertically to a wall (necessarily a façade wall) between the windows, which latter should give, if possible, a north light. Rooms below such a laboratory would show supports for large furnaces and rooms above must allow the ventilating chimneys to pass. In a physical laboratory the blackboard occupies a most important position.

Laboratories in general must be large and afford plenty of space for the work in hand. When a study necessitates the carrying from place to place of cumbersome objects, passages must be very conveniently arranged. Ventilation should be abundant.

For microscopic work, the laboratory becomes merely a long gallery, with windows descending to the level of the work table and giving north light directly thereupon. If, on account of peculiarities in the general plan, it becomes necessary to place such a hall north and south, the lighting is made bilateral, and a screen placed down the middle of the hall that students can work with a west light in the morning and cross over to an east light in the afternoon. Tables for microscopic work must not be susceptible to vibrations.

Another complement of the lecture hall is the museum of collections; this is especially necessary in connection with medical and anatomical studies, as well as for natural history and geology. If the lighting is unilateral the depth of the museum should not exceed twenty-five feet. The substitution of light from above for lateral lighting is unsuccessful, both in

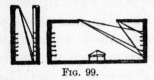
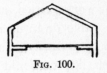

FIG. 99.   FIG. 100.

point of lighting and ventilation. If no windows are feasible, arrange the cases of shelves that the light which strikes them will be as inclined as possible. For this reason a skylight should not cover the whole ceiling. The cases must stand under dark portions of the latter; therefore the room must be made low and wide. A glance at Fig. 99 will explain this. Shelves which come one above the other ought to be of glass, so that only specimens will cast a shadow. The lower shelves may be successively placed farther out to get more light.

Halls having a skylight (Fig. 100) need exterior

and interior frames of glass (in roof and ceiling) to form an air space and prevent the hall below from becoming overheated. The outer glass is clear glass, but that in the ceiling, ground. For cleaning measures, a solid space must be left as a passage below the roof and around the glazed portion of the ceiling. Moreover, the space between the ceiling and roof should have openings connecting it with the outer air. This gives ventilation, preventing an accumulation of heated air and carrying off the moisture which would otherwise condense on the panes. The tendency of vapor to condense is often an annoyance to the architect. It is necessary in cold climates to provide a means of carrying off any water which may collect and run down the inclined under side of outer frames. Another possibility which it is well to keep in mind is the breaking out of putty which cements the glass into its iron frames, caused by the difference of expansion between glass and iron. When an exterior skylight is ugly in façade, it may be kept on the inner side of the building; this is usually adequate for lighting purposes. A skylight, however, often gives character to a roof.

Before leaving the question of schools, we may say a word about studios and some special institutions of learning which have not the usual kind of class room. Painters' and sculptors' studios are more or less square, because the students work from models. Light here is best, both vertical and horizontal, from the north. Some painters like an east or northeast light. The heating should be concentrated near the model stand, so at the side opposite the light. Models' dressing rooms should connect with such studios. Sculptors' studios are to be kept on the ground, on account of the weight of the clay; otherwise intermediate supports below the floor would be necessary. Architects' studios are long rooms or galleries, with unilateral north light. There must be depots of boards and stretchers.

Music rooms should not be on the street, on account of noise from each.

Dissecting rooms, in medical or art schools, call for windows on all four sides, giving complete means of ventilation. Special arrangements for running water are to be made.

Work rooms in manual training schools and shop rooms in general are to be well lighted by lateral and, if possible, vertical light, and must be especially adapted to the kind of study. As for laboratories, plenty of space is a requisite.

For riding schools, etc., the ring or riding hall is well made rectangular. The best average proportion is width equal to about one third of length. Light must be diffused, so that the horses will have no shadows at which to shy. No projections in the hall below seven feet eight inches. The lower portion of the walls may have a batter, preventing the legs of equestrians from being scraped or crushed by unruly horses. The entrance is best on the small side of the rectangle, to give a rider time to control his horse after entering the ring. A riding hall must be very well ventilated. Horses are mounted outside the ring.

BUILDINGS OF GENERAL PUBLIC INSTRUCTION

Museums, Picture Galleries, Libraries, etc.

There are two usual methods for connecting the exposition rooms of museums or picture galleries; viz.: that of the single circulation and that of the double circulation (Fig. 101). The former is better

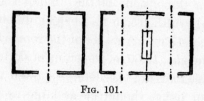

FIG. 101.

when objects are exposed only around the walls of the room; the latter, when objects are also in the middle of the room. In general, arrange the suite of rooms so that a visitor may see the whole collection without retracing his steps or having recourse to a guide book.

Interior decorations of an exposition room should be absolutely simple; nothing must detract from the objects on view. The Pitti Palace of Florence and the Louvre were not made for picture galleries, thus, despite the art displayed, are not successful as such, though a room destined for the reception of certain very modern exhibitions might admit of noticeable decoration, so that the visitor could be sure of something agreeable on which to rest his eyes. In lecturing on the "Theory of Architecture" at the Ecole des Beaux Arts, M. Guadet advised the students not to attempt to decorate a room in the style of the exhibit it is to contain. Such imitations are always sure to result disastrously, for the reproduction will conflict with the original; and were not this the case, the original would have no background to set it off. In the judgment of the Cairo museum, designs which affected Egyptian decorations were, *a priori*, discarded.

In museums and picture galleries excessive height is bad. The height should be approximately equal to the width. The interior dimensions of the "Salon Carré" of the Louvre are: width, 15.75 m.; height, 19.60 m.; width of skylight, 5.47 m. Another of the rooms has: width, 17.45 m.; height, 15.50 m.; opening of skylight, 8.23 m. Both of these halls are excellently adapted to their use. The exterior lights should be as large as possible; of greater area than the openings in the ceiling of the hall.

In libraries the reading room must be well lighted by a diffused light — no shadows to be tolerated. Stack rooms, too, need thorough lighting. The height of stacks is divided by galleries into stories, each about seven feet high in the clear. The floors of these galleries

FIG. 102.

are made of glass. Fig. 102 shows two arrangements, the first having an opening between galleries, the second openings between a central gallery and the books. The open spaces in the latter case are closed with a wire mesh, to prevent books from falling to the bottom of the stack room.

THEATERS AND OPERA HOUSES

Such buildings are always to be divided into two distinct parts, for the public and the actors. Between

s

these should be a heavy wall, that a fire arising amid the scenery may not endanger the public; this wall, too, may insure the saving of the greater part of the house.

The entrance and exit become our first study. The carriage approach must not interfere with that of arrivals on foot. If the building is in a street block, those who drive will alight on the sidewalk, and everybody will enter in the same way. The architect will merely have to arrange a marquise over the sidewalk. (Of course, the carriages must not drive over the sidewalk, even to pass under the building to an interior porte cochère; such an arrangement would block the sidewalk.) But if the building is isolated, with streets on all sides, then, perhaps, the best solution is that of lateral marquises (sometimes objected to, because not monumental) or more architectural porte cochères. The latter are to be so arranged that, at the same time, several carriages may stand under cover and receive their occupants, and any one of the carriages be able to emerge from the line and drive off, although the first ones remain in place. The scheme of driving under the theater has been tried, but not found successful, because of draught and rumbling, audible in the auditorium. A waiting room is an accessory of the porte cochère; likewise, a waiting vestibule for the attendants and footmen.

In entering the house and during entre-actes, the public is able to appreciate the effect of the vestibules and staircases in a manner not possible during the hurry and crowding of exodus. It is logical, then, to adopt the plan of the Opera House of Paris, where the public arrives, and ascends to the main parts of the house by elaborate vestibules and a monumental staircase, and leaves by a great number of staircases, continuations to the ground floor of the smaller staircases used from the main part of the house (the floor where the foyer is) to the upper floors of the second, third and fourth galleries. Following this theory in detail, we should make all doors of the public portion of the house open outward. If a panic occur, the natural sequence to an alarm of fire, this precaution is of utmost importance. As to the special arrangements of minor staircases, a number of comparatively narrow ones, side by side, are better than a single one with wide steps. People like to use the handrail, and in a crowd those coming down on the outside have farther to go around the turns than those on the inside, while those on the inside may be crushed together and forced over the first step after the landing. There should be no winders in a staircase which a crowd of people is to use. The landings on the different floors must be quite independent of the halls and passages, in order to allow those on point of descending to pause without obstructing the passage.

The foyer is naturally a place for the artist to display his skill in decoration. It is well to place the foyer at about the height of the first balcony or between the levels of the back of the pit and the balcony.

As to the auditorium itself, the best shape, combining advantages for seeing and hearing, is that of the somewhat elongated horseshoe. By referring to

what has already been said with regard to lecture
halls, we understand why the deeper hall is better for
sound than the half circle. The depth of a theater
or opera house auditorium should be at least equal to
the breadth (Fig. 103, A, $d \gtreqqless b$).

In determining the height of the successive rows

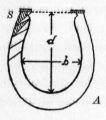

of seats we must make one addition
to our previous suggestions respect-
ing more semicircular halls. Since
theater auditoriums are elongated,
and actors often at the back of the
stage, farther removed from the
center of the circle of the balconies, a
spectator at a' (Fig. 103, B) looking
at o', will see over the point b', instead of over b_1. $a'b_1$ being less than
ab' and the height of points in the
same row being the same, $a'b_1$ or $a\,b$,
which has a like inclination, will be
less near the horizontal than will
$a'b'$. So, while a spectator at a can
see o', those at a' may *not* be able.
Therefore the height of the rows

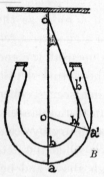

FIG. 103.

must be calculated along such lines as $a'b'$. We may
feel assured that if conditions on the side of the house
are satisfactory those in the center will be.

Loges with high sides should only be placed in the
middle of the house, as persons in the back of a box
on the side can see nothing. In Fig. 103, A, the shaded
portion of the box at S is quite useless, as far as catching a glimpse of even the middle of the back of the

stage is concerned. Never make supports in the audience hall of a theater. Balconies must be supported by brackets or in cantilever.

As to the shape of the stage, although the impression from the house is one of depth, this is really illusory. The stage ought to be very wide, at least three times the width of the opening of the proscenium arch; but depth is of less consequence. Indeed, too great depth is bad, the voice being lost in the back, while the scenery, which might act as a sounding board or reflector, is not near enough to the opening of the curtain to be useful. Effects of perspective are better obtained by painted scenery.

It is well, if possible, to place such a room as the "foyer de dance," on axis, behind the stage, arranged in such a way that it can be thrown open at the end and used, on occasion, to increase the actual depth. This becomes most acceptable in ballet scenes, when the front of the stage must be given up to the dancers.

The great width of stage is made necessary by scenery stored there ready to be drawn on when the acts change. There must be height enough above and below the opening of the stage to raise and lower scenery out of sight.

Capacity of the heating apparatus need not, comparatively speaking, be very great, as the exterior passages keep the auditorium from cooling off. The influx of warm air must not be concentrated in one place. Ventilation can never be too great; the stage is especially difficult to ventilate well without sudden changes of temperature. In any case, there should be automatic openers connected with the different skylights above the stage, so that all will open conjointly and may be managed from a central point during the entre-actes.

Lighting of the house should be diffused. A chandelier kept high is admissible and, moreover, decorative. Stage lights are never to be seen by the audience. A double system of lights should exist, so that if one fails, the second will be in reserve. Water is carried to points over the stage, to be used in case of fire.

Adjuncts of the stage are store rooms, dressing rooms of the artists, dancers, etc., musicians' rooms, the "foyer de dance," green room and library. Moreover, there should be a group of offices, belonging to the administration, and ample provision for machinery, etc.

Governmental or Administrative Buildings

Architecture of such buildings should be dignified in character, typifying the power of the nation or state whose laws or decrees are therein conceived and carried out. In America our State Capitols have already struck the note of an appropriate style, strong in its classical derivation and well poised, although possessed of little originality. Our court houses and prisons are somewhat less successful. American architects, striving after the new, have often turned either to the old or to the curious; unwilling to use a Classical Renaissance, they have taken to the Early Renaissance or to the grotesque. To be sure, the most attractive and beautiful specimens of the Rathaus and Hotel de

Ville are to be found in old Germany and old France; and as long as a Rathaus or Hotel de Ville is desired, perhaps we can do no better than copy or, to use a less harsh word, draw inspiration therefrom. But in America we have a civilization differing materially from that of the sixteenth century, and it takes a real genius to adapt, without making an unfortunate "pastiche," the architecture of another land and time to our own. The difficulty of using an old style in governmental work is shown even more when the especial building has no counterpart in an earlier epoch. Thus prisons of to-day, built to resemble Egyptian temples or mediæval battlemented fortresses, never look as if for our workaday world.

The requirements of a State Capitol are of two groups: comprising rooms frequented by the public, and those not open to them. Of the latter the large chambers of the House and Senate may allow of some suggestions. The question of acoustics must be studied in such a way as to allow of members speaking in any part of the hall and being heard throughout. A semi-circular hall of 100 feet diameter is a good maximum; a larger hall is tiring to the voice. Light in the back of galleries for the public is unnecessary and occasions difficulty in the exercise of supervision over those admitted. The heating should come from several points, and light must also be diffused. An artificial lighting, tried in such halls, was the arrangement of lights above a ground glass skylight; this proved expensive.

Court rooms are best planned with unilateral lighting; skylights cast unnatural shadows and are not

agreeable. Sills of windows should be six feet from
the floor, that no one can look out. Of course, no
lateral passages or galleries may cut the light from
the windows of the court room. Accused and wit-
nesses should be placed with faces to the light; the
jury may be against the light. The judge must not
face the light nor have light behind him, as he would
be thereby prevented from seeing and being seen.
The judge would naturally be in the axis of the court
room, and at the end opposite the entrance. Vaulting
in a court room would reverberate too much.

Prisons are to be divided into two distinct parts:
for the service and for the prisoners. Especially to
be guarded against are places available for hiding,
gathering for escape or the preparation of outbreaks.
Prisoners are not to mingle, except in accordance with
special rules. From one work room they should not
be able to see or communicate with prisoners in another, and it is particularly important that they be
not able to see outside the prison. All cells are to be
isolated, that tapping on the wall of one cannot be
heard in the next, there are to be no projections; vaulting is good. The entrance to a prison is best made with
a court between a first and second set of doors. This
allows carriages to drive into an inner court without
there ever being an open communication between it
and the exterior.

COMMERCIAL BUILDINGS

Our commercial buildings are so peculiar in their
requirements that it is especially difficult to give any

general suggestions. A new program must be made out for each case. No practical consideration should be disregarded or slighted; it is by giving to each its full value that character will be attained.

In office buildings, built as an investment of money, no waste space is to be tolerated. The best method to follow in composing the exterior is (see "Scale," on page 66) to include several stories in base courses and several in the cornice. Great arches are usually not acceptable, as they make bad windows for the interior. The entrance, elevators and corridors demand most careful study.

Large stores, where the whole building is devoted to one business, must be very light; no superfluous stone piers or imitation piers to limit the show windows. It must be kept in mind that vapor will condense on the interior of the panes of closed, unventilated and heated show windows.

Factories must also have the maximum of light. All of these buildings must be fireproof.

Railroad stations are to be divided into two groups: terminal and nonterminal, or way stations. In such buildings the question of the circulation of the public becomes most important. In Europe an arrangement exists (as in the Gare St. Lazare of Paris) where the public is only permitted free entrance to a long hall, *a* (Fig. 104, *A*), placed perpendicularly to the lines, and separated therefrom, or rather, from a second open space, *b*, which connects the ends of the lines by waiting rooms, *w*. In America a more practical system unites these two open spaces, the waiting rooms

being elsewhere (*B*, Fig. 104); such is the case in the
Pennsylvania Railroad station in New York, in the
Grand Central station in New York, in the Southern
Central station in Boston, etc. In large terminal sta-
tions the suburban lines are sometimes separated from
the main lines; a general division may also be made

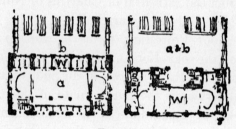

FIG. 104.

between arriving and departing lines. A free choice
between these systems usually does not rest with the
architect. He must aim to obviate the blocking of
traffic and to enable the traveler to find his way without asking questions. The latter, discovering himself
in the wrong place, should be able, in minimum time,
to rectify his mistake. In general, the whole plan
should be an open one.

ECCLESIASTICAL BUILDINGS

A last chapter in our study of different buildings
is the interesting one pertaining to ecclesiastical architecture. There are two extremes toward which such
buildings tend: the mystical and the scientific. Of
the former the Roman Catholic church is a type; of
the latter, the ethical culture cults. The more worship tends to the mystical, the more do forms, pageants,

processions, impressive ceremonies, music and all that appeals to the senses, and through them to the imagination, become important; as the cult tends to the scientific, the more are these, are any suggestion of aught greater than force and matter, excluded.

Character must foreshadow these tendencies. The range is from the cathedral of Chartres or Notre Dame de Paris to the ethical lecture hall.

None of our Protestant forms of worship has the fullness of the old Roman Catholic service. In all modern services there is need of an auditorium. The Episcopal service is the most ornate of these. While it is the direct descendant of the English and earlier Roman Catholic service, it usually shows no need for processions. In the planning of its churches it does away with the requisite of side aisles and even chapels, substituting that the greatest number of worshipers must hear and follow the priest, both in sermon and service. It is true that the Church of England holds its services in old cathedrals; but this is, in spite of their want of adaptation, evidenced by the greater part of the English churches being closed off by choir screens, etc.

The practical requirements are changed in the most conservative of our forms of modern worship. Is the spirit changed also?

Certainly, some divisions of the Church of England are not far removed from the old feeling at Rome, but the great body is essentially modern. In our churches it is a mistake to copy old cathedrals in plan — present needs are changed; a fault to imitate them in feeling — modern spirit has forgotten the old.

The architect who has a place of worship to build must imbue himself with the thought and feeling of the worshipers. He must be practical when a lecture hall is needed — the speaker in the axis, with seats circling around, no column to obstruct the view (this is true in all modern churches), good acoustics, good ventilation, good light. In spirit he must be a pantheist when asked for a temple, a ritualist when asked for a cathedral.

He will find no worshipers in the old mediæval sense — culture is come and "the people" are departed. His consolation is in the thought that if the gentle twilight of the past is gone, at least day, not night, is taking its place.

INDEX OF SUBJECTS

INDEX OF PROPER NAMES

272

THE following pages contain advertisements of a few
of the Macmillan publications on kindred subjects

Design in Theory and Practice

By Ernest A. Batchelder, Author of " Principles of Design." Profusely illustrated. Decorated cloth, gilt top. 291
pages.

Net, $1.75; postpaid, $1.90.

This work is in no sense an effort to formulate a system or method
for teaching design, but is rather the presentation of the problems
and the ideas that have gradually developed during many years of
teaching and practice. It will prove a helpful book not only to
teachers and students who may be directly interested in the subject,
but to the many others who feel the lack of a criterion or standard
to assist them in forming a judgment in question of design.

A judgment is of little value unless it can be backed with a logical
reason; hence we may consider as pertinent any serious discussion
which aims to define the principles of design and their practical application, touching upon a more sane, more artistic production, on the
one hand, and a more intelligent, more discriminating judgment on
the other. This is best accomplished by the presentation of a series
of problems. In setting mind and hand to the solution of a definite
problem we meet and overcome questions which no amount of reading can foresee. The problems in this book lead from the simple,
constructive use of lines and forms under clearly defined limitations
to work involving considerable invention, fine feeling, and freedom
of execution. They begin with the geometric and work toward Nature; with the abstract, coming gradually into closer relation with the
constructive questions discussed in the different chapters of the book.

Over two hundred diagrams and illustrations are given, of designs
used in wood, metals, leather, pottery, etc., the examples ranging
from the ancient tombs of Eygpt and the basketry and blankets of
the North American Indians to the most elaborate and exquisite
specimens of Greek and modern workmanship.

"The author conducts us through a series of problems leading from the
simple, constructive use of lines and forms under clearly defined limitations to work involving considerable invention, fine feeling, and freedom
of execution." — *The Independent.*

THE MACMILLAN COMPANY
Publishers   64–66 Fifth Avenue   New York

The Decorative Illustration of Books

By WALTER CRANE

Decorated cloth   12mo $2.00

The author's purpose is to treat of illustrations which are also book ornaments, so that purely graphic design, as such, unrelated to the type, and the conditions of the page, does not come within his scope.

The Bases of Design

By WALTER CRANE

Decorated cloth   12mo $2.25

The chapters in this book originally formed a series of lectures addressed to the students of the Manchester Municipal School of Art during the author's tenure of the directorship of Design at that institution.

Decorative Heraldry

By G. W. EVE

Decorated cloth   12mo $2.00

It was with a view to assist in some measure the efforts that in so many directions are being devoted to the adequate presentation of Heraldry that this work was undertaken.

Design for Schools

By CHARLES HOLLAND

Decorated cloth   Illustrated   Quarto $1.90

A handbook for teachers for use in secondary schools, the upper standards of elementary schools and elementary classes of schools of art.

PUBLISHED BY

THE MACMILLAN COMPANY

64-66 Fifth Avenue, New York

Heraldry for Craftsmen and Designers

By W. H. ST. JOHN HOPE, Litt. D., D.C.L.

With diagrams and illustrations, mostly from ancient sources, and also collotype reproductions and colored plates.

Cloth, 12mo. Preparing.

For more than twenty-five years the author of this volume has been secretary of the Royal Society of Antiquaries, and he is held to be one of the leading authorities on all that pertains to heraldry. Owing to the importance of the subject — the wide and revived interest that is being taken in it in this country, and the appeal that it will undoubtedly make to every craftsman and designer as well as to many general readers — the work is certain of a cordial reception, as it is really the first to be published which is both complete and inexpensive.

THE MACMILLAN COMPANY

Publishers   64-66 Fifth Avenue   New York

THE ARTISTIC CRAFTS SERIES

Embroidery and Tapestry Weaving

Second Edition

By Mrs. A. H. CHRISTIE

178 diagrams and illustrations by the author.   16 pages
of collotype reproductions.   320 pp.

$2.00 net; postpaid, $2.15

EXTRACT FROM "THE PALL MALL GAZETTE"

"Mrs. Christie has performed her task to admiration . . . and her lucid
explanations of various kinds of stitches . . . should be of value to all
workers at embroidery or tapestry weaving and to novices anxious to learn."

Writing and Illuminating, and Lettering

Third Edition

By EDWARD JOHNSTON

227 illustrations and diagrams by the author and Noel
Rooke.   8 pages of examples in red and black.   24
pages of collotype reproductions.   512 pp.

$2.00 net; postpaid, $2.14

EXTRACT FROM "THE ATHENÆUM"

". . . This book belongs to that extremely rare class in which every
line bears the impress of complete mastery of the subject. We congratulate
Mr. Johnston on having produced a work at once original and complete."

THE MACMILLAN COMPANY

Publishers   64-66 Fifth Avenue   New York

Hand-Loom Weaving

By LUTHER HOOPER

125 drawings by the author and Noel Rooke. Coloured and collotype reproductions. 368 pp.

$2.25 net ; postpaid, $2.38

EXTRACT FROM "THE MORNING POST"

". . . Every phase and process in weaving is described with so clear and careful an exactitude that, helped as the text is by the author's sketches and diagrams, the reader should have no difficulty in conquering with its aid the rudiments of the craft."

PORTFOLIOS (IN THE SERIES) ALREADY ISSUED

School Copies and Examples. Selected by W. R. Lethaby and A. H. Christie. 12 drawing copies (1 in colours), with descriptive letterpress. *$1.25 net*

The animals and Italian woodcuts in this series make available for school purposes fine works of art in facsimile, and also bring together examples carefully chosen as being educational and suggestive.

Manuscript and Inscription Letters

For Schools and Classes and the Use of Craftsmen. By Edward Johnston. With 5 plates by A. E. R. Gill, 16 plates in all. Full Notes and Descriptions by the Author. *$1.25 net*

THE MACMILLAN COMPANY

Publishers   64-66 Fifth Avenue   New York

ST. MARY'S COLLEGE OF MARYLAND LIBRARY
ST. MARY'S CITY, MARYLAND